OPEN YOUR MOUTH!

WHAT TO SAY
WHEN SHARING
THE GOSPEL

MARK A. MATHEWS
foreword by ROBERT L. MILLET

CFI, an imprint of Cedar Fort, Inc.
Springville, Utah

For Joseph and for Bruce

ISBN 13: 978-1-4621-1892-2

Published by CFI, an imprint of Cedar Fort, Inc.
2373 W. 700 S., Springville, UT 84663
Distributed by Cedar Fort, Inc., www.cedarfort.com

LIBRARY OF CONGRESS CATALOGING-IN-PUBLICATION DATA

Names: Mathews, Mark A., 1978- author.
Title: Open your mouth! : what to say when sharing the gospel / Mark A. Mathews.
Description: Springville, Utah : CFI, an imprint of Cedar Fort, Inc., [2016] | ©2016 | Includes bibliographical references and index.
Identifiers: LCCN 2016008192 (print) | LCCN 2016009730 (ebook) | ISBN 9781462118922 (perfect bound : alk. paper) | ISBN 9781462126750 (epub, pdf, mobi)
Subjects: LCSH: Evangelistic work--Church of Jesus Christ of Latter-day Saints.
Classification: LCC BX8661 .M324 2016 (print) | LCC BX8661 (ebook) | DDC 266/.9332--dc23
LC record available at http://lccn.loc.gov/2016008192

Cover design by Shawnda T. Craig
Cover design © 2016 Cedar Fort, Inc.
Edited and typeset by Sydnee Hyer

Printed in the United States of America

10 9 8 7 6 5 4 3 2 1

Printed on acid-free paper

CONTENTS

CONTENTS

FOREWORD

Many years ago, my friend and colleague (and at the time the dean of Religious Education at BYU), Robert J. Matthews, made this comment: "It's almost inevitable that people who want to proclaim that they have the truth, that theirs is the path to salvation, seem always to be just one dispensation behind the times." I wasn't quite sure what he meant, and so Bob explained that in the meridian of time the Savior declared the gospel, organized His Church, and, in company with His Apostles, invited men and women to come unto Him to be saved. The response of those who were offended by His message, who spurned His witness that He had come to reveal the Father, was that they already had Moses and the law, that they were descendants of Abraham, that they needed no man to teach them (JST Matthew 7:14). That is, they were stuck in an earlier dispensation, whether the Abrahamic or the Mosaic; they were looking backward rather than forward and their allegiance was to dead prophets, legal administrators of a former time.

And so it is in our own day. As Latter-day Saints go into the world to declare the message of the restored gospel, whether members or full-time missionaries, they are frequently met by persons who reject their message in the name of what they already have in the Holy Bible. "I have Jesus; that's all I need," as one woman said to me recently. At the April 1974 general conference of the Church, Elder Bruce R. McConkie addressed himself to this phenomenon:

> We be Abraham's children, the Jews said to Jove [Jehovah];
> We shall follow our Father, inherit his trove.
> But from Jesus our Lord, came the stinging rebuke:
> Ye are children of him, whom ye list to obey;
> Were ye Abraham's seed, ye would walk in his path,
> And escape the strong chains of the father of wrath.
> We have Moses the seer, and the prophets of old;
> All their words we shall treasure as silver and gold.
> But from Jesus our Lord, came the sobering voice:
> If to Moses ye turn, then give heed to his word;
> Only then can ye hope for rewards of great worth,
> For he spake of my coming and labors on earth.
> We have Peter and Paul, in their steps let us trod;
> So religionists say, as they worship their God.
> But speaks He who is Lord of the living and dead:
> In the hands of those prophets, those teachers and seers,
> Who abide in your day have I given the keys;
> Unto them ye must turn, the Eternal to please. (Bruce R. McConkie, in Conference Report, April 1974, 100–101)

Jedediah M. Grant, who served for a time as a counselor to President Brigham Young, said, "When you read of the gifts that were bestowed upon and circulated among the people of God, you certainly would not wish others to suppose that mere reading about them puts you in possession of the same blessings." President Grant continued: "But many in the world would suppose that when they preach and circulate the Bible, they actually put in the possession of the people that power and life and those gifts, that the ancient apostles and Prophets and Saints of God enjoyed." He then made this remarkable observation: "Brethren and sisters, *we understand the difference between enjoying and reading of enjoyment, between the history of a feast and the feast itself;* also between the history of the law of God and the law itself" (Brigham Young, *Journal of Discourses,* 4:18; emphasis added).

Further, because of this reaction on the part of persons of other faiths, we as Latter-day Saints are tempted to confine ourselves to the

Bible in our earnest but misguided effort to "prove" the Restoration. To be sure, there are biblical passages that are allusions to great doctrinal truths, but so very often these are only allusions. Frankly, we do not as a people practice baptism for the dead, for example, because of 1 Corinthians 15:29. Nor do we teach that there are three degrees of glory hereafter because of either John 14:1–2 or 1 Corinthians 15:40–42. We teach such doctrines because these matters were revealed to the Prophet Joseph Smith and because of the scriptural justification found in the Book of Mormon, Doctrine and Covenants, Pearl of Great Price, and the sermons and writings of latter-day prophetic successors to Brother Joseph. To be clear on this matter, Latter-day Saints love the Bible. It is holy scripture, the word of God, one of the books within our scriptural canon. It is a member of the royal family of scripture, and we do not love one member of the family more than another. If we wanted, as an illustration, to teach about the Sermon on the Mount or to discuss the Master's Bread of Life sermon, we would certainly turn our attention to the New Testament.

But those doctrines that are unique to the Restoration, those powerful teachings to us and to all of God's children that come through the instrumentality of modern prophets, go beyond what the Bible delivers. (To supplement is not to supplant.) They broaden and deepen our understanding of the Father's plan of salvation, enunciate priceless insights concerning the immortality of all men and women, uncover priceless gems of doctrine concerning the nature and necessity of the priesthood, explain what temples are and why the Almighty desires His people to receive covenants and ordinances there that can be had nowhere else, provide supernal perspective on the eternal continuation of the family, and clarify the origin and destiny of the human family—what we may become. For these most distinctive insights we must turn to the scriptures of the Restoration.

We are indebted to Mark Mathews for providing in this important book a solid and significant reminder that we as a people must stay in context, the context of restored truth; that the glad tidings we are charged to declare are "the things which have been revealed to [God's] servant, Joseph Smith, Jun." (D&C 31:3–4); and that the only way that we may be free from the condemnation, scourge, and judgment that comes from treating lightly what we have received is to bear testimony "to all the world of those things which are communicated unto [us]"

(D&C 84:54–61). This book sets forth the manner in which all members of The Church of Jesus Christ of Latter-day Saints, no matter their station in life or their educational attainment, may open their mouths, may feel confident in inviting others to hear our unique message, and may bear witness with an assurance that the same Lord that called Joseph Smith and restored His gospel and His Church is the Lord that will assist you and me as we seek to share what we have.

The Holy Spirit will guide and empower our words. We have every reason to believe that our sincere efforts will succeed.

—Robert L. Millet,
professor emeritus of ancient scripture,
Brigham Young University

INTRODUCTION

I love missionary work. I remember at the end of my mission in Guatemala being asked by some of the younger missionaries what I would miss the most about my missionary service. As I pondered that question, I realized that many of the things that I loved the most about missionary work I would still be able to do when I returned home. I would still be able to study the scriptures and pray in faith. I would still get to serve in the Church and teach the gospel (even do so professionally as an employee of the Church Educational System). And, of course, I would still be able to share the gospel sometimes as a member missionary.

But what I remember feeling at that moment was that, while I still would be able to do all of those things I loved, I would no longer be able to do them with the same intensity and single-minded devotion as I could as a full-time missionary. I would have work and family obligations. There would be distractions.

And so the answer I gave was simple: What I would miss the most about being a full-time missionary was *being a full-time missionary*. I would miss that feeling of knowing that I was completely consecrated to the work of the Lord; that I was called by a prophet to serve twenty-four hours a day, seven days a week; that, as my nametag indicated, I was a full-time representative of Jesus Christ. That is what I miss the most. That feeling of complete consecration is indescribable to me. I still have moments when I wish I could wake up one more day in Guatemala, put on those old beat up dress shoes, slip on the missionary nametag that meant everything to me, and walk out that front door as a full-time servant of the Lord. I loved being a missionary.

These were the memories and feelings that came back to me in June 2013 when I was gathered with Saints in locations all over the world to hear a Church broadcast about hastening the work of salvation. In that historic meeting, President Thomas S. Monson proclaimed, "Now is the time for members and missionaries to come together, to work together, to labor in the Lord's vineyard to bring souls unto him" ("Faith in the Work of Salvation," *Ensign*, October 2013, 38). The message I heard from that meeting was clear. No longer were we as members of the Church to be content just praying for the full-time missionaries—*we were to be full-time missionaries*, fully engaged in the work of finding, inviting, and fellowshipping. I felt like I had once again been called to labor in the full-time service of the Lord by a prophet of God! I walked out of that meeting filled with a familiar spirit, the spirit of missionary work, which is the Spirit of the Holy Ghost.

But not every member of the Church is so excited to do missionary work. For some, especially those who have not yet had the opportunity to serve a full-time mission, sharing the gospel can be an intimidating thing, even a dreaded topic they don't want to talk about. As Elder M. Russell Ballard explained, "We know that when someone gets up to give a talk in sacrament meeting and says, 'Today I'll be talking about missionary work,' . . . some of you listening may think, 'Oh no, not again; we have heard this before'" ("Put Your Trust in the Lord," *Ensign*, November 2013, 44). One reason I have observed for this reluctance to participate in missionary work is that many Church members just don't know what to say. There are so many things that we believe and practice in the Church that it can be overwhelming, and many would-be member missionaries are left confused and even a little scared about what they should say in missionary opportunities.

I believe that the simple solution to this problem is found in catching the vision of the Restoration. The message of the Restoration is that through revelation the gospel of Jesus Christ was restored through the

Prophet Joseph Smith. This simple message is fundamental to our religion. In fact, all of our many unique beliefs and practices in the Church grow out of the Restoration, and so this ought to be the first thing we instinctively share when sharing the gospel. This message gives direction, guidance, and order to all that we share as missionaries. Not only that, but the better we understand the message of the Restoration, the more we will appreciate what we have to offer the world and the more we will want to share it. Likewise, the better we communicate the message of the Restoration, the more others will recognize the importance of what we have and the more they will want to hear it. Member missionaries do not need to feel scared or confused about what to say; they just need to have the confidence to share the message of the Restoration.

Unfortunately, however, there are many members of the Church who have not yet caught the vision of the Restoration and, as a result, do not always represent our message well. Some seem to think that missionary work is about convincing people that our Church is just like the church they already belong to. They seem so determined to focus on common beliefs and emphasize our similarities that they fail to appreciate the unique and powerful message that we have to declare to the world—that the fulness of the gospel has been restored and it is the only hope of salvation in the latter days!

One former mission president expressed my feelings perfectly on this matter when he said,

> The message of the Restoration centers in the idea that it is not common ground we seek in sharing the gospel. There is nothing common about our message. The way we answer questions about our faith ought to be by finding the quickest and most direct route to the Sacred Grove. That is our ground. It is sacred ground. It is where the heavens are opened and the God of heaven speaks. It is where testimonies are born and the greatest truths of heaven are unveiled. It is of this sacred ground that we say, here we stand. (Joseph Fielding McConkie, *Here We Stand* [Salt Lake City: Deseret Book, 1995], 6)

I was taught this powerful principle as a young missionary in the MTC and it has been an inspiration and a guide to me ever since. I believe it has everything to do with why I feel so strongly about missionary work today. This lesson reminds us that as important as it is to let people know that we are Christian, that alone is not enough in our missionary efforts. If we spend all of our time explaining what we're *not*—some strange cult—then we will miss the opportunity to explain who we really are: the *true* Church of Jesus Christ. Remember, the purpose of missionary work is not just to convince the world that we are Christian; it is to convert the world to Christ's true Church. In doing so, it is not enough for us just to share how we are similar to other churches; we must also share what makes us different and sets us apart from all the other Christian churches. It is in these differences that the strength of our position is found. These differences are what attract people to our Church and inspire them to join. These differences begin with the First Vision and grow out of the Restoration. They are what make this "the only true and living church upon the face of the whole earth" (D&C 1:30).

The purpose of this book is to expound on this concept. My objective is not to explain *how* to do missionary work by providing specific examples of member missionary experiences. Rather, the purpose of the book is to provide perspective and direction about *what* to share and *why*. My hope is that this will help us catch the vision the Lord has revealed for missionary work, a vision that centers in the First Vision and embraces the message of the Restoration. The principles taught are basic and fundamental but also deep and profound and not always fully appreciated.

This book is written to members of the Church, young and old, regardless of missionary experience. For those preparing for full-time missionary service, I remind you of the counsel of Elder David A. Bednar, that "the single most important thing you can do to prepare for a call to serve is to *become* a missionary long before you go on a mission" ("Becoming a Missionary," *Ensign*, November 2005, 45). Becoming a missionary is more than just putting on a white shirt and a nametag; it is about becoming the type of person who loves the restored gospel and loves the people around them enough to want to share it with whoever will listen. Becoming a missionary is about gaining the heart of a missionary and having the spirit of missionary work. You can accomplish this by catching the vision of the Restoration of the gospel of Jesus Christ.

For the rest of us who are not currently called to serve full-time missions, I remind us of the counsel of Elder Neil L. Andersen, "If you're not a full-time missionary with a missionary badge pinned on your coat, now is the time to paint one on your heart—painted, as Paul said, 'not with ink, but with the Spirit of the living God'" ("It's a Miracle," *Ensign*, May 2013, 77). We "paint" that missionary badge on our hearts when we catch the vision of the Restoration.

It is my hope that these words will inspire us to catch the vision of the message of the Restoration in missionary work and have the courage to share not only what makes us similar to other churches, but what sets us apart. The world needs the restored gospel of Jesus Christ, and the Lord is counting on us to share it with them. Because He is counting on us, we can count on Him to assist each of us in opening our mouths and sharing the message of the Restoration.

1

THE MESSAGE OF
THE RESTORATION

What do members of your Church believe?" At some point in our lives each of us will hopefully be asked that important question. It is helpful to think about how we would respond to missionary opportunities so that when they unexpectedly come, we can "be ready always to give an answer to every man that asketh [us] a reason of the hope that is in [us]" (1 Peter 3:15). As it says in the scriptures, "if ye are prepared ye shall not fear" (D&C 38:30).

For many of us, even when we are prepared, it can still be a little scary. But if we have prepared and if we try our best, the Lord has a way of helping us through these missionary opportunities (see D&C 84:85). Sometimes it is "in the very moment" that he inspires us as to "what [we] shall say" (D&C 100:6). My wife Mandy had such an experience the summer before we were married. Her experience has been teaching me ever since. She recalls:

> During spring term at BYU, I had the opportunity to participate in a study abroad experience in London, and I flew out of the Salt Lake International Airport on a Monday morning in April. I boarded the plane and took a seat next to two women who looked like they were in their fifties. These women were on their way from South Carolina

to Chicago and had a layover in Salt Lake. We exchanged pleasantries, and then I was getting settled when a group of about twelve missionaries walked onto the plane. One of the women asked the other who this group of boys in suits were, and she replied that she didn't know. She asked me if I knew, and I answered that they were missionaries for The Church of Jesus Christ of Latter-day Saints, the "Mormons" as they are sometimes called. She looked surprised and asked me if I knew any Mormons. I laughed and said, "Actually, I *am* a Mormon." She smiled and responded, "Oh really? I'm a Catholic. I have heard a little about your Church, and it seems like you really aren't that different from the Catholics. Don't Mormons have quite a bit in common with us?"

The Potential Problem of Focusing on Common Beliefs

Before we continue this story, we need to consider how to respond to this preliminary question. Think about it for a moment. Why would a good missionary be hesitant to agree that our Church has so much in common with another church? Why might a good missionary be careful to avoid those efforts that would minimize our differences and magnify our similarities? What would have happened if my wife had simply agreed with the woman's question and stated that our Church was just like hers?

Instinctively, my wife understood that not only *are* there important differences in our churches, but to say otherwise would destroy this golden missionary opportunity. Had my wife simply agreed, then the conversation would have most likely ended right there, because why would anyone be interested in knowing what we believe if they think it is the same as what *they* believe? They already know what they believe, and so there is no reason to find out more.

There is a very important lesson in this that every missionary should know. People don't search for what they've already found. No one investigates what they already know. Sometimes we as members of the Church become so concerned about people thinking we are "weird" that we are afraid to stand out and be different. We end up sacrificing missionary opportunities in an attempt to fit in. We try to convince others that our Church is just like theirs, not realizing that by so doing we not only stifle their curiosity, but we also give them no reason to join us. Because why would they want to join a new church that is just like the one they already belong to?

A simple analogy helps us quickly see the problem. Imagine you are a vacuum cleaner salesman trying to sell a new vacuum with this approach. "Here is this new vacuum, and it is just like the one you already have. How many would you like to buy?" It doesn't take much sales experience to recognize why that approach wouldn't work very well. And it doesn't work well in missionary work either. As missionaries, we are not salesman, but the principle is the same. We want to help people see that we have something different to offer, something unique that cannot be found in any other church.

Unfortunately, many missionaries don't realize that emphasizing common beliefs rather than our unique message can unintentionally convince people *not* to investigate the Church. One mission president witnessed an unfortunate illustration of this. He related, "The missionaries had an investigator present. He was a very intelligent and fine man who was active in the Catholic faith. During the meeting the branch members did everything they could think of to convince this man that we, as Latter-day Saints, were just like him. They succeeded. At the end of the meeting he got up, walked out the door, and never came back. He told the missionaries on the way out he could see no reason to leave an established church to join one that was trying so hard to be just like what he already had" (Joseph Fielding McConkie, *Here We Stand*, 5).

This story dramatically illustrates the potential problem with the missionary approach of "building on common beliefs"—it is that we rarely do any building! Too often this approach simply means establishing common ground by emphasizing what we have in common without ever sharing what we have to offer that is different. Such an approach may be helpful at making friends and allies for the church, but it will not make many converts. Remember, as "the only true and living church" we are unique (D&C 1:30). By definition, we can't be the only true Church and at the same time be like everybody else. And we must never be afraid to proclaim our differences from other churches, because those very differences are what set us apart as the only true Church. These differences are what draw people to our Church and inspire them to join it. What every missionary should know is that that "conversion comes from the differences and not the similarities. The reason people join the Church is because you show them the differences between us and the world" (Bruce R. McConkie, "Book of Mormon Seminar," BYU June 3, 1984).

Fortunately, my wife had good missionary instincts and gave a great response. She acknowledged our similarities, but she didn't stop there. She then emphasized that there are also things in which we are different from other churches, hoping that they might feel compelled to find out more. Those differences are what people want to know about. Those differences are what give us a message worth sharing and worth hearing. They are what paved the way for what happened next. Mandy explained, "I answered that while we do share a few basic beliefs, our church is actually quite different from the Catholic church. She was obviously surprised by my answer, and then asked, 'Really? So what do members of your church believe?'"

What do members of your church believe? What a great question! It is a question every good missionary wants to hear. It is an open-ended, perfect missionary opportunity. So, how do we respond? What do we say about what we believe?

Laying the Foundation of the Restoration

When I have put my seminary students on the spot and had them answer this question from a potential investigator, I have received many different responses. Some of the more typical responses have included the Articles of Faith, the plan of salvation, the Book of Mormon, the Atonement and gospel of Jesus Christ, Joseph Smith, living prophets, and eternal families. I have always been impressed with their responses. They seem to know instinctively what missionaries should talk about because all of these are found in the missionary lesson plans. But where should we start? What should we teach first? Where do we begin when we frankly don't know what to say? As Mandy struggled to give a response, she experienced the Lord's promise to give us "in the very moment, what [we] shall say" (D&C 100:6). It was then that the Lord taught her a valuable lesson in sharing the gospel. She explains:

I had my triple combination in my backpack, so I pulled it out. I showed her the Book of Mormon, but my first instinct was to take her to the Articles of Faith, because they all start with "we believe." I showed them to her, but without any context or foundation, it was like jumping into the middle of a lake. She didn't really get it, and the conversation almost died right there. It simply didn't work. That was when I realized that I needed to start at the beginning. I needed to teach her about the Restoration, and so I began telling the story of the First Vision.

It is a common response to take investigators immediately to the Articles of Faith in missionary work, but the potential problem with this is that it attempts to explain what we believe without explaining *why* we believe it. Without any context or foundation, this gives the impression that we are "jumping into the middle of a lake," as my wife expressed it. What the Lord taught her that day is something every missionary should know. It is not enough for us to simply explain *how* we are different; we must explain *why* we are different. And to do that requires us to share the message of the Restoration, which is that the fulness of the gospel of Jesus Christ has been restored through a modern prophet named Joseph Smith.

As missionaries, we are like builders constructing a house of gospel understanding for our investigators. Wise builders always begin by laying a proper foundation. Unwise builders assume that the foundation someone already has will be sufficient to carry the weight of their new house. This is why unwise missionaries assume they can build on common ground, independent of the message of the Restoration, but wise missionaries always lay that foundation. They know that without the foundation that comes from the message of the Restoration, our doctrines and beliefs won't make as much sense.

In fact, the Articles of Faith prove this very point. Though we typically think of them today as a separate and distinct list of beliefs, they were not originally written to stand alone. They come from a famous letter Joseph Smith wrote in 1842 to a newspaper editor named John Wentworth. The intent of the letter was to explain who we are as a church and what we believe. It concluded with thirteen statements of belief known today as the Articles of Faith. These statements are helpful in missionary work because they bring the investigator quickly and powerfully to many of our distinctive beliefs and should be relied on heavily. But it is important to remember that they came at the *end* of the letter, not the beginning.

Before Joseph Smith shared the Articles of Faith, he taught the Restoration. In fact, the Wentworth letter begins with an abbreviated version of Joseph Smith—History. Only after laying a foundation of the key events of the Restoration did Joseph Smith begin to explain our beliefs, because he understood that no meaningful understanding of what we believe can be had independent of the knowledge of *why* we believe it. We can't fully appreciate the fruits of our faith until we understand the roots of our religion.

All of our distinctive beliefs grow out of the Restoration. We believe what we believe because there has been a restoration. That is why the Articles of Faith so perfectly follow Joseph Smith—History in our scriptures and why they should follow the message of the Restoration in our missionary discussions as well. Before we share what we believe, we must first declare why we believe it. And that means we must begin with the message of the Restoration, as Joseph Smith perfectly illustrated in his own example of missionary work.

The Pattern of Joseph Smith—History

As a learning activity, I sometimes ask my mission preparation class to rank the standard works in order of their importance to missionary work. Typically the lists they come up with have two things in common: they begin with the Book of Mormon and end with the Pearl of Great Price. The students are shocked when I then inform them that the Pearl of Great Price is just as important as the Book of Mormon in missionary work and belongs next to it, at the top of the list, tied for first place.

I don't immediately tell them why this is the case because I want them to struggle with it and discover the reason for themselves so they will remember it better. After a few seconds of wrestling, a student always comes to the rescue and shares a simple answer that reunites the class into perfect agreement. The reason why the Pearl of Great Price is so important to missionary work is because it contains Joseph Smith—History.

When one realizes what Joseph Smith—History is and to whom it is written, immediately it becomes apparent how valuable of a resource this is in missionary work and why we must never overlook this important book. In the first verse, Joseph Smith states that he is writing specifically to "inquirers after truth," or what we would today call investigators (Joseph Smith—History 1:30). This means that Joseph Smith—History is basically a missionary tract written to investigators by Joseph Smith acting as a missionary (and it is still used today as a missionary pamphlet). It is the classic example of how Joseph Smith, over time, came to share the gospel, making it an invaluable resource in missionary work and a perfect pattern to follow. If you have ever wondered how the

Prophet Joseph Smith would share the gospel, Joseph Smith—History is the answer.

In Joseph Smith—History, the Prophet begins sharing the gospel by teaching the key events of the Restoration. These events are the First Vision (JS—H 1:1–26), the coming forth of the Book of Mormon (1:27–67), and the restoration of priesthood authority in order to organize the Church (1:68–75). These are the most fundamental events of the Restoration, and they lay the foundation of all that we believe and all that we teach as missionaries. They are what Joseph Smith taught first as a missionary, and they are what we should teach first as missionaries.

The importance of beginning with the message of the Restoration is confirmed by *Preach My Gospel: A Guide to Missionary Service*, which trains missionaries to follow the pattern of Joseph Smith—History and begin missionary discussions by teaching these same key events of the Restoration. Though the format may change, the importance of declaring these fundamental truths remains the same. As missionaries, we should instinctively follow Joseph Smith's example in responding to investigators by teaching them the First Vision, the Book of Mormon, and the restoration of the priesthood and Church.

By beginning with the message of the Restoration, we lay a foundation for everything else we teach. Again, *Preach My Gospel* illustrates this perfectly by the order in which missionary lessons are presented. It is only after we have taught the message of the Restoration that we can effectively teach the plan of salvation and the gospel of Jesus Christ, because our knowledge of those things comes from the Restoration. It is because of the Restoration that we understand more clearly the role of Jesus Christ and the terms and conditions of salvation set forth in His gospel. Without the light and knowledge that have come to us through the Restoration, we would have nothing more to teach the world on those subjects than what they already have.

Our Commission

Teaching message of the the Restoration has always been our commission as missionaries. This is perfectly illustrated in one of the early mission calls of this dispensation. In September 1830, Thomas B. Marsh was called to serve with these classic words of instruction, "Lift up your heart and rejoice, for the hour of your mission is come; and your tongue shall be loosed, and *you shall declare glad tidings of great joy unto this generation*" (D&C 31:3; emphasis added). The phrase glad tidings literally translates to "good news" and was first used in the scriptures when angels announced the birth of Jesus Christ (see Luke 2:10). The phrase is used here to teach us a valuable lesson. The birth of Christ was the good news of *that* day, but what is the good news "unto this generation" that we are to declare? The Lord explained that in the next verse: "You shall declare the things which have been revealed to my servant, Joseph Smith" (D&C 31:4). The things revealed to Joseph Smith are the events and revelations of the Restoration. What this means is that the good news we are sent out to declare in our day is the message of the Restoration.

It is for this reason that missionaries are called not just to teach the gospel. Specifically, their commission is to teach the *restored* gospel. For example, when missionaries receive their call to serve in the mail, they are often so excited to read where and when they will serve that they stop reading the letter before they learn what they are actually called to do. The letter states, "You have been recommended as one worthy to represent the Lord as a minister of the restored gospel." This distinction of teaching the *restored* gospel is so important that, to make sure we don't miss the point, it is restated and explained on the first page of *Preach My Gospel*. There, as the primary explanation of our purpose as missionaries, we are told, "Your commission [is] to teach the restored gospel of Jesus Christ," meaning, missionaries are to teach "the gospel of Jesus Christ as *restored through* the Prophet Joseph Smith" (*Preach My Gospel* (2004), 1; emphasis added).

The gospel includes all of the truths, laws, principles, and ordinances that all mankind must believe and obey in order to be saved by the Atonement of Christ (see Articles of Faith 1:3–4). As messengers of salvation and witnesses of Christ, true missionaries always teach the true gospel. But our commission is something more. Specifically, we are instructed to teach the *restored* gospel, which we cannot do without teaching the message of the Restoration. This means that we are not just to teach faith, repentance, and baptism; we are to teach these gospel principles in the context of the Restoration and explain that our knowledge of these things and authority to teach and practice them come because of the Restoration. We must show the world not just that these things were known anciently and revealed through the Bible, but also that they have been revealed again and restored in our day through the Prophet Joseph Smith. That is what it means to teach the restored gospel, and understanding this commission is central to our role as missionaries.

In fact, this is exactly what the phrase "preach my gospel" means (D&C 50:14). It means that we are commissioned to preach the *restored* gospel. This is implied in the fact that the phrase itself comes from Doctrine and Covenants 50, making it a *latter-day revelation from Jesus Christ*. To preach *His* gospel means more than simply teaching the world about Christ and His Bible teachings; it means we are sent to teach them what Christ has revealed in our day. The title *Preach My Gospel* is a constant reminder that we are sent out to teach "the gospel of Jesus Christ as restored through the Prophet Joseph Smith" (*Preach My Gospel*, 1).

When You Don't Know What to Say

What all of this means for us as missionaries is that we should train ourselves to instinctively share the message of the Restoration of the gospel of Jesus Christ. We should be Restoration missionaries. When asked about our faith, if we don't know what to say, we should begin with the message of the Restoration. This was the counsel of one Apostle to another as Elder Mathias Cowley instructed his son, future Apostle Matthew Cowley, before he left on his first mission:

> I will never forget the prayers of my father the day that I left [on my mission]. I have never heard a more beautiful blessing in all my life. Then his last words to me at the railroad station, "My boy, you will go out on that mission; you will study; you will try to prepare your sermons; and sometimes when you are called upon, you will think you are wonderfully prepared, but when you stand up, your mind will go completely blank." I have had that experience more than once.
>
> I said, "What do you do when your mind goes blank?"
>
> He said, "You stand up there and with all the fervor of your soul, you bear witness that Joseph Smith was a prophet of the living God, and thoughts will flood into your mind and words to your mouth, to round out those thoughts in a facility of expression that will carry conviction to the heart of everyone who listens." And so my mind, being mostly blank during my five years in the mission field, gave me the opportunity to bear testimony to the greatest event in the history of the world since the crucifixion of the Master. Try it sometime, fellows and girls. If you don't have anything else to say, testify that

Joseph Smith was the prophet of God, and the whole history of the Church will flood into your mind mind [and] the principles of the gospel. (Matthew Cowley, *Matthew Cowley Speaks*, [Salt Lake City: Deseret Book, 1960], 298–99)

This advice is timeless. To testify of Joseph Smith is to testify of the Restoration of the gospel of Jesus Christ. Unless we receive some special inspiration to the contrary, we should begin our missionary conversations with the message of the Restoration, just as Joseph Smith showed us (see JS—H 1:1–75) and as *Preach My Gospel* directs us to (see *Preach My Gospel*, 30–31). By providing the foundation and context to everything we teach, the Restoration becomes the springboard, launching us into further discussion. As Elder Cowley explained, "the whole history of the Church will flood into [our] mind" (Matthew Cowley, *Matthew Cowley Speaks,* 298). To do otherwise, as my wife discovered, can have the opposite effect. It can actually hinder our expressions and impede our missionary conversations by failing to lay the proper foundation— "jumping into the middle of a lake" as she called it.

The message of the Restoration propels further conversation not only because it lays the foundation but also because it brings the Spirit of the Holy Ghost. Missionaries everywhere can attest to the special spirit and power that attends the testimony of Joseph Smith and the Restoration of the gospel of Jesus Christ. As Elder Cowley explained, "Thoughts will flood into your mind and words to your mouth, to round out those thoughts in a facility of expression that will carry conviction to the heart of everyone who listens" (Matthew Cowley, *Matthew Cowley Speaks,* 298). To testify of the Restoration will bring as much power and inspiration today as it did then, and it always will.

This is why prophets and apostles continue to stress the importance of sharing the message of the Restoration to all the world. President Gordon B Hinckley counseled, "Let us reach out to the world in our missionary service, teaching all who will listen concerning the restoration of the gospel, speaking without fear but also without self-righteousness, of the First Vision, testifying of the Book of Mormon and of the restoration of the priesthood" ("A Time of New Beginnings," *Ensign,* May 2000, 87). And as President Dieter F. Uchtdorf has shared, "As members of the Church of Jesus Christ, we have a responsibility to extend the message of the restored gospel of Jesus Christ, as guided by the Spirit, to every corner of the world" ("Truth Restored," BYU Campus Education Week, August 22, 2006).

The Restoration Is a Message about Jesus Christ

As we teach the Restoration, there will no doubt be some inside and outside of the Church who question and even criticize this direct approach by asserting that we should talk more about Jesus Christ and less about the Restoration. I once had a seminary student who made this very objection in class. We were discussing the Restoration and the importance of declaring it in missionary work. Behind me on the screen was a large image of the First Vision. The young man asked me if it wouldn't be better to talk about Jesus Christ first rather than the Restoration when we share the gospel. I smiled and pointed to the image of the First Vision and asked, "What do you see in this image?" He quickly responded, "Yeah, I know, I see Joseph Smith and the First Vision, but I'm asking, shouldn't we focus on Christ?" Again I smiled, pointed to the image and slowly asked, "Yes, but who else do you see in this image, besides Joseph Smith?" This made him pause and reflect for a moment. You could actually see him catch the point I was trying to make. He then looked back at me and thoughtfully said, "I see Jesus Christ. I think I understand now what you are saying."

This beautiful teaching moment illustrates a point that everyone who shares the gospel needs to understand—to teach and testify of the Restoration is to teach and testify of Jesus Christ. For example, when we testify of Joseph Smith's First Vision, we are testifying of Jesus Christ, who appeared in that Sacred Grove. When we testify of the coming forth of the Book of Mormon, we are testifying of Jesus Christ, whose testament that book is. When we testify of the restoration of the priesthood and the Church, we are testifying of Jesus Christ, whose priesthood and Church it is.

We must never lose sight of this simple fact. To build on the foundation of the Restoration is to build on the rock foundation of Jesus Christ, for it is His gospel and Church that has been restored. Therefore, when we stand with Joseph Smith in the Sacred Grove and on the Hill Cumorah and on the banks of the Susquehanna River (where the key events of the Restoration took place), we are standing with Jesus Christ on the foundation He has laid in the latter days. It is only through the foundation of the Restoration that anyone is truly and fully built on the rock of Christ today (see D&C 10:69). Simply stated, we come unto Christ today through the Restoration.

Therefore, we must all strive to be Restoration missionaries and lay the foundation of the Restoration in missionary work. As a church, that is where we stand, and it is where our converts must learn to stand also. As *Preach My Gospel* directs, "No matter where you serve or whom you teach, center your teaching on the Restoration of the gospel of Jesus Christ. 'The Lord will bless you as you teach the message of the Restoration to a world that desperately needs the gospel of Jesus Christ' ("Statement on Missionary Work," First Presidency Letter, 11 Dec. 2002). As you study the doctrines in the missionary lessons, you will come to see that we have one message: Through a modern prophet, God has restored knowledge about the plan of salvation, which is centered on Christ's Atonement and fulfilled by living the first principles and ordinances of the gospel" (Preach My Gospel, 6).

2

THE FIRST VISION FIRST

I will never forget the lesson I learned as a young missionary in the MTC. It was a large Sunday School meeting. The instructor was a BYU religion professor. Because he was the son and grandson of two well-known Church leaders who were heroes of mine, my district had been teasing me all morning that I should get his autograph. I didn't. But I did pay careful attention as he spoke. I can't remember all that he said in that lesson; in fact, all I remember is what he said about one verse of scripture, but that one verse changed my life as a missionary and revolutionized the way I viewed sharing the gospel.

The verse he shared was from Joseph Smith—History. It is Joseph Smith's description of how he reacted to the invitation to "ask of God" in James 1:5. It states,

> Never did any passage of scripture come with more power to the heart of man than this did at this time to mine. It seemed to enter with great force into every feeling of my heart. I reflected on it again and again, knowing that if any person needed wisdom from God, I did; for how to act I did not know, and unless I could get more wisdom than I then had, I would never know; *for the teachers of religion of the different sects understood the same passages of scripture so differently as to*

destroy all confidence in settling the question by an appeal to the Bible.
(JS—H 1:12; emphasis added)

Instead of focusing our attention on the first part of the verse, where most people concentrate, this teacher drew our attention to the last part and pointed out a phrase that I had overlooked before. After describing the influence of the spirit of revelation on his soul, the Prophet Joseph offers this insightful, parenthetical thought: "For the teachers of religion of the different sects understood the same passages of scripture so differently as to destroy all confidence in settling the question by an appeal to the Bible." The "question" Joseph is referring to in this verse is the question that had been on his mind for so long, that is, "Which church is true?" In this moment, Joseph realized something that had never occurred to him before, and has still not occurred to enough of us. The answer to the question will never be settled "by an appeal to the Bible," because "the same passages of scripture" are interpreted "so differently" (JS—H 1:12; see also Jeffrey R. Holland, "My Words . . . Never Cease," *Ensign*, May 2008, 92).

That message entered *my* heart with great force that day and caused me to reflect on it then and ever since. The Bible, because it is interpreted so differently by so many, will never adequately settle the question of which church is true. This may be the single most important verse of scripture that any missionary can understand about how to effectively share the gospel. When properly understood, it influences the way we do missionary work forever. Let me explain.

Prior to this point in my life, I thought that missionary work was a matter of comparing Bible verses. I naïvely assumed that the Bible was common ground and that Bible believers had a common understanding of what the Bible means. I don't know how I had come to such a mistaken conclusion, having grown up in the "Bible Belt" of Texas, but I naively expected that I would get out to the mission field and point out what I assumed were obvious evidences in the Bible that our Church was true, and those who believed the Bible would be so impressed with these verses that they would join the Church. "Wow, Elder Mathews! I've never seen that verse before. . . . Can I be baptized?" Or something to that effect.

As a result, I had felt a little inadequate as a missionary because I was not an expert on the Bible and felt limited in my ability to build on common beliefs and find common ground. Frankly, I was not sure how well I had memorized all the seminary scripture mastery verses aimed at "proving" the Church true from the Bible.

Sadly, it had never occurred to me that if which church was true were so obvious from the Bible, there wouldn't be so much confusion and so many thousands of different Christian churches—and each of these churches is one more proof that the Bible alone cannot establish which church is true. If it were so obvious from the Bible, we wouldn't need missionaries and we wouldn't need Restoration; all we would need is for everyone to read the Bible and come to the same conclusion and join the unity of the Christian faith. But that is not at all what actually happens, and this experience in the MTC helped me see that. I realized with Joseph Smith that, try as we might, we can't successfully identify which church is true from the Bible because everyone interprets it differently. Because people can't agree on what the Bible means, they can't agree on which church is true by using the Bible alone. If Joseph Smith couldn't discover which church was true from the Bible alone, what hope do our investigators have in doing so? The answer simply is not there, and it never was.

If the answer is not found in the Bible, where then can it be found? Again, Joseph Smith gives the answer, "Unless I could get *more wisdom* than I then had," he explained, "I would never know" (JS—H 1:12; emphasis added). The only way to know which church is true was to get "more wisdom," but where could he get more wisdom than that which is in the Bible? The answer is simple. It is the answer that so powerfully impacted Joseph Smith. The way to gain more wisdom was to "ask of God" and receive it by revelation (James 1:5). What Joseph Smith discovered that day, and what every missionary should know, is that the answer to the question, *"Which church is true?" is not found in the Bible, but in latter-day revelation.* Specifically, God answered the question in the First Vision.

This is the simple realization that changed my life as a missionary. I knew then what I had to do. Instead of ineffectively trying to prove the Church true from the Bible, I would follow the counsel of Joseph Smith and rely on latter-day revelation to determine which church is true. Rather than simply offering them different interpretations to scripture they already have, I would offer them "more wisdom" or in other words, more revelation—latter-day revelation. Specifically, if my investigators wanted to know which church was true, I would take them in the quickest and most direct route to the Sacred Grove. There, I would let God Himself answer the question through the First Vision. Then I would invite them to follow the example of Joseph Smith and ask God if it were true.

Teaching the First Vision First

The first lesson of Preach My Gospel is entitled "The Message of the Restoration of the Gospel of Jesus Christ." Underneath that title is found a beautiful print of a painting by Greg Olsen. It is a depiction of the Sacred Grove. I assume that it is there to remind missionaries that the essence of that first lesson, the central-most important message it contains, is the First Vision. It is a constant reminder that, as missionaries, we teach the First Vision first.

Teaching the First Vision first, meaning as part of the first lesson in missionary work, is nothing new. It has been part of the first discussion since the Church began producing standardized missionary lesson plans. Even before that, it was often the pattern of the Prophet Joseph Smith to begin missionary discussions with the First Vision (e.g. Joseph Smith—History and the Wentworth letter). The missionaries in his day followed that example. In Scotland and Germany, Apostles Orson Pratt and Orson Hyde each published an account of the First Vision to use as a missionary tract in those countries. From the earliest days of the Church, it has been a pattern of missionary work to teach the First Vision first.

From a certain point of view, this pattern was set even before the missionary efforts of Joseph Smith and his contemporaries. An experience with a seminary student taught me that. One day after an assembly, a young man came up to me and explained that he had been thinking a lot about something we had discussed the previous day in class. Then he asked me who the first missionaries of this dispensation were. Not realizing this was a rhetorical question, and thinking I was really smart, I responded that traditionally we give that honor to Samuel Smith, Joseph's brother. As I gave this response, though, I could tell there was something on his mind that he wanted to share, so I asked him why he wanted to know. He then offered one of the most beautiful insights into missionary work I have ever heard. The first missionaries of this dispensation were Heavenly Father and Jesus Christ, he said. Their first investigator was Joseph Smith, and Their first lesson was the First Vision. Then he explained that, as missionaries, we should follow Their perfect example by teaching the First Vision first.

As he shared this, I was deeply moved by this insight. It brought new meaning to all those times I taught the First Vision with my missionary companion. In a very real way, we were representing the Father and the Son as we echoed Their words to those investigators. They could not come in person to instruct each investigator about which church is true, so They spoke once to Joseph Smith, and then They sent us to carry that message to all the world. To this day, when I look at paintings of the Father and Son visiting Joseph Smith, I sometimes can't help but imagine them wearing missionary nametags.

Teaching the First Vision first in missionary work is nothing less than the pattern set by God Himself when He taught Joseph Smith. It was the pattern of the Prophet Joseph Smith and the early missionaries of this dispensation. It is the pattern set by every organized lesson plan ever developed by the Church, including Preach My Gospel. We would be wise to follow this example and teach the First Vision first. "There is no better place to start," said President Boyd K. Packer, "than with the First Vision" ("The Only True Church," *Ensign*, November 1985, 81).

Why We Teach the First Vision First When Sharing the Gospel

But what is it about the account of the First Vision that makes it such a powerful place to begin in missionary work? As you read the following summary of this sacred event, assume the roles of a missionary and an investigator and consider from their perspectives why the First Vision is such a perfect place to start.

In his own words, the Prophet Joseph Smith explained,

There was in the place where we lived an unusual excitement on the subject of religion. . . .

I attended their several meetings. . . . But so great were the confusion and strife among the different denominations, that it was impossible for a person . . . to come to any certain conclusion who was right and who was wrong. . . .

While I was laboring under the extreme difficulties caused by the contests of these parties of religionists, I was one day reading the

Epistle of James, first chapter and fifth verse, which reads: If any of you lack wisdom, let him ask of God. . . .

I reflected on it again and again. . . .

At length I came to the conclusion that I must either remain in darkness and confusion, or else I must do as James directs, that is, ask of God. . . .

It was on the morning of a beautiful, clear day, early in the spring of eighteen hundred and twenty. . . .

After I had retired to the place where I had previously designed to go, having looked around me, and finding myself alone, I kneeled down and began to offer up the desires of my heart to God. . . .

I saw a pillar of light exactly over my head, above the brightness of the sun, which descended gradually until it fell upon me. . . .

When the light rested upon me I saw two Personages, whose brightness and glory defy all description, standing above me in the air. One of them spake unto me, calling me by name and said, pointing to the other—*This is My Beloved Son. Hear Him!*" (JS—H 1:5, 8, 11–17)

With those seven simple words, God the Father introduced His Son, Jesus Christ, to the Prophet Joseph Smith. Joseph's humble prayer was answered. Through this experience and others, the question of "Which church is true?" was answered by latter-day revelation. The answer is The Church of Jesus Christ of Latter-day Saints. Only this Church administers salvation and offers the true path to heaven.

Now, consider why we, as missionaries, would want to teach the First Vision first.

Perhaps the most basic answer is that the First Vision is exactly what its name implies: it is the first revelation of this dispensation, and so we teach it first is because it is first. The First Vision was the Lord's introduction to the Restoration, His official announcement to all the world that His gospel and Church would be restored. Where better to begin to tell our story than at the beginning?

Because it is the first revelation of this dispensation, the First Vision also becomes the foundation of the Restoration. All the revelations and blessings of the restored gospel are based upon it. Without it, there would be no Book of Mormon, no priesthood, no ordinances, no true church (see James E. Faust, "The Magnificent Vision Near Palmyra," *Ensign*, May 1984, 68). Indeed, as the soil of the Restoration, all that we believe and all the good we have in the Church grows out of the Sacred

Grove, as the "fruits of the First Vision" (Dieter F. Uchtdorf, "The Fruits of the First Vision," *Ensign*, May 2005, 36; see also Gordon B. Hinckley, "Pursue the Steady Course," *Ensign*, January 2005, 3).

By teaching the First Vision first, we lay this same foundation for our investigators and prepare them to receive and enjoy all the blessings and teachings that grow from it. In fact, accepting the First Vision as truth prepares a person to accept all the other truths of the Restoration and the other teachings missionaries share. As President Joseph F. Smith expressed, "The greatest event that has ever occurred in the world, since the resurrection of the Son of God . . . was the coming of the Father and of the Son to that boy Joseph Smith, to prepare the way for the laying of the foundation of his kingdom. . . . Having accepted this truth, I find it easy to accept every other truth that he [Joseph Smith] annunciated and declared" (*Gospel Doctrine*, 495–96).

As a result of its status as the introduction to and the foundation of the Restoration, the truthfulness of our message rests, in large measure, on the First Vision. President Gordon B. Hinckley powerfully reminded us of this when he said, "Our entire case as members of The Church of Jesus Christ of Latter-day Saints rests on the validity of this glorious First Vision. It was the parting of the curtain to open this, the dispensation of the fulness of times. Nothing on which we base our doctrine, nothing we teach, nothing we live by is of greater importance than this initial declaration. I submit that if Joseph Smith talked with God the Father and His Beloved Son, then all else of which he spoke is true. This is the hinge on which turns the gate that leads to the path of salvation and eternal life" ("What Are People Asking about Us?" *Ensign*, November 1998, 71; see also "The Great Things Which God Has Revealed," *Ensign*, May 2005, 81).

As President Hinckley so boldly expressed, our whole message rests on the validity of the First Vision. It is either true or it is not. And we testify that it is true, and because it is true, everything else that has grown from it is also true. Because so much depends on it, accepting the First Vision becomes an initial test to determine our salvation. President Marion G. Romney said, "Upon our acceptance and testimony to the truth of this vision . . . hangs our individual salvation" (*Learning for the Eternities* [Salt Lake City: Deseret Book, 1977], 8; as quoted by Howard W. Hunter, "Hearing and Heeding the Message of the Grove," *Ensign*, February 2009, 10).

By teaching the First Vision first, we get right to the point, and we quickly determine who is interested in the restored gospel and prepared to receive it. It immediately separates the wheat from the tares. As Elder Jeffrey R. Holland explained, "Nothing in our history or our message cuts to the chase faster than our uncompromising declaration that Joseph Smith saw the Father and the Son and that the Book of Mormon is the word of God" (*Christ and the New Covenant* [Salt Lake City: Deseret Book, 2009], 346).

Another reason to share the First Vision first is that it answers so many questions about our Church. For example, there are some who ask if we are Christian and if we believe in the Bible. The First Vision is the perfect response to these questions because it was Christ's true Church that the young Joseph was seeking, and it was the Lord Jesus Christ Himself who appeared to him in response to that search. It also responds to the question of the Bible, showing plainly that we believe the Bible, for it was the Bible that inspired Joseph to "ask of God" (James 1:5). No one who has heard and understood the First Vision needs to wonder about our faith in Christ or our belief in the Bible.

But of course, it doesn't stop there. The First Vision not only shows our similarities, it also reveals those truths that set us apart. We teach some of our most unique and powerful doctrines when we teach the First Vision first. For example, we learn that God is a personal being, in whose image we are created; that He is separate and distinct from His Son; that the Lord can speak today by modern revelation to living prophets; and that there had been an apostasy from the New Testament Christian church (see Tad R. Callister, "Joseph Smith—Prophet of the Restoration," *Ensign*, November 2009, 35–36; Robert D. Hales, "Receiving a Testimony of the Restored Gospel of Jesus Christ," *Ensign*, November 2003, 28). All this stands in stark contrast to the teachings of traditional Christianity.

In fact, because it so powerfully reveals some of our most unique and treasured doctrines, the First Vision becomes the summary and symbol of our whole message. Our message to the world is that there is a God in heaven, that Jesus Christ is His Son, that They live and speak today to living prophets, and that through these latter-day revelations They have restored the true gospel and Church to the earth. All of this is dramatically revealed in the First Vision and is yet another reason to teach the First Vision first.

But there is another, more personal reason for why we do this. The First Vision is the universal story that every investigators can relate to and learn from. By teaching the First Vision first, we perfectly demonstrate to them how they can find out for themselves which church is true. They must "ask of God" (James 1:5). When they ask God, just like Joseph Smith, they will come to know, just like Joseph Smith.

Not only does the First Vision show investigators how to receive an answer to their prayers, it is the answer to their prayers. God is an efficient revealer. "It is contrary to the economy of heaven for the Lord to repeat to each of us individually what he has already revealed to us collectively" (David M. McConkie, "Gospel Learning and Teaching," *Ensign*, November 2010, 15). Instead of revealing the same message to everyone independently, God's pattern is to reveal it once to a prophet and then confirm it to everyone else by the power of the Holy Ghost (see Moroni 10:3–5).

What many fail to realize is that this is exactly what He has done with the First Vision. The First Vision was not just a personal revelation *to* Joseph Smith; it was a latter-day revelation through Joseph Smith to all of us. If anyone wants to know which church is true, God's answer *to them* is the First Vision. And He will confirm it personally by the power of the Holy Ghost.

A beautiful illustration of this is found in an experience my wife had with a co-worker at a part-time job at BYU. She recalls,

> I began working as an operator shortly after I became engaged, and one evening when calls were few and far between, I began talking with a couple of other operators who were also engaged. We were comparing wedding plans and which temples we were going to be married in, and my friend mentioned that she would be married in the Logan Utah Temple, but she was sad because her family wouldn't be able to come. This sparked my curiosity, and I asked her a few questions. In the course of the conversation, she explained that she was the only member in her family, and her parents were disappointed that they would be unable to attend her marriage ceremony. Despite the difficult family situation it placed them in, she and her fiancé remained firm in their decision to marry in the temple. She said that she had joined the Church when she was a young teenager, to the great dismay of her family, and they had never really accepted her decision fully. I asked if she would share her conversion story, and, like many

converts, she was excited to do so. She said that when she was about fourteen or fifteen years old, she began to wonder which church was true and felt compelled to find it. She attended all of the different denominations in her area, but none of them ever felt quite right. She even researched some non-Christian religions, such as Buddhism, but again, they didn't feel right, and as time went by she almost gave up. One day, she was on the Internet when she recalled that at one time she had a friend who was a member of the "Mormon" Church. She searched for "Mormons" on the Internet and was led to the Church's website. Through a link on that site, she was led to the account of the First Vision found in Joseph Smith—History. She read it with tears in her eyes and an unexplainable feeling in her heart, because *Joseph's* story was *her* story, and she felt that somehow he had shared her same feelings and many of her experiences, and he had found the answer she was seeking. Right there, in front of the computer, she knew that she had found the true Church, and soon thereafter she called the missionaries to find out how to join.

This powerful story perfectly illustrates the point. The First Vision was not meant for Joseph Smith alone. When Joseph Smith went into the woods that day, he did not go alone; he went as the representative of untold millions who would one day ask the same question and, through him, get the same answer. His search is their search. And as they kneel with Joseph in their own Sacred Grove, they will come to know that his answer is their answer, as God speaks again from the heavens, confirming to them His message to Joseph Smith. By the power of the Holy Ghost, it can be for them as if they had experienced the First Vision personally.

Elder John K. Carmack shared an experience that further illustrates this point: "I was reviewing the account of the First Vision," he explained, when he had "a singular experience. There came to me a very, very special witness that what was recounted by Joseph Smith . . . was exactly what happened. In a sense, I experienced, as it were, the First Vision myself. And I became a witness to it, a personal witness, through the power of the Holy Ghost. I bear you that witness that the Father and the Son did appear to Joseph Smith the Prophet. I imagine that my experience was very similar to that which many of you have had" ("Upheld by the Prayers of the Church," *Ensign*, May 1984, 75–76).

This leads us to one more reason to teach the First Vision first: it brings the Spirit. Because so much depends on this story being true, we can be assured of one thing—God will give us power to teach it. My experiences, and the experiences of countless other missionaries, is this: I never had more power than when I taught the First Vision. There were moments when the Spirit of the Holy Ghost was so strong that it felt as if the Father and the Son had just appeared to us, for we were in Their presence.

As missionaries, we follow the example of the Father and the Son, and of Joseph Smith and of many early missionaries, by teaching the First Vision first. Whenever missionary opportunities arise, we should make it a priority to share with our friends the story of the First Vision. We teach the First Vision first because it introduces and lays the foundation for the Restoration. We teach the First Vision first because, as President Hinckley said, if it is true, then it is all true (see "What Are People Asking about Us?" 71). We teach the First Vision first because it identifies some of our similarities with other churches, while emphasizing those truths that set us apart and make us the only true Church. We teach the First Vision first because it shows our investigators the only way they can ever know which church is true. We teach it first because, if taught with conviction, it brings power and testimony. There may be some preliminary things we teach to set the stage. One might be prompted to address a particular need of an investigator or explain the apostasy or role of prophets as *Preach My Gospel* suggests, but our primary introductory message to all the world is the First Vision. That is why we teach the First Vision first and why we should always be "First Vision" missionaries. We invite all to come unto Christ today through the Sacred Grove.

The message of the Restoration centers in the idea that it is not common ground we seek in sharing the gospel. There is nothing common about our message. *The way we answer questions about our faith ought to be by finding the quickest and most direct route to the Sacred Grove.* That is our ground. It is sacred ground. It is where the heavens are opened and the God of heaven speaks. It is where testimonies are born and the greatest truths of heaven are unveiled. It is of this sacred ground that we say, *here we stand.* (Joseph Fielding McConkie, *Here We Stand*, 6; emphasis added)

3

THE BOOK OF
MORMON SECOND

I **have always** been a student of the Book of Mormon. As a
child, I remember being taught the Book of Mormon stories by my
mother. When I was old enough to read, I set out to finish it on my
own and did so when I was eleven years old. I continued to study it in
seminary and throughout high school and college, so that by the time
I entered the MTC, I had read it several times. Though I had read the
Book of Mormon multiple times, I had never once thought to pray to
ask God if it were true. It simply never occurred to me to ask. And I
might never have done so were it not for the pressure I began to feel in
the MTC. And so one afternoon, finding myself alone in my room (a
rare thing in the MTC), I knelt down by my bed and asked God if the
Book of Mormon were true.

I asked in faith and expected a response, but not the response I
received. The message that came to me was simple and direct. Only in
time would I recognize how profound it was. The message that came to
my mind and heart was this: "Mark, you know the Book of Mormon is
true. You've always known it is true. Now, get off your knees and start
testifying of the Book of Mormon."

As I applied that inspired counsel in my own missionary efforts, standing and testifying of the Book of Mormon, my appreciation and love for that book grew more and more. I began to see why Joseph Smith immediately followed his testimony of the First Vision with an explanation of the Book of Mormon and why *Preach My Gospel* instructs us to do the same (see *Preach My Gospel*, 37–38). Now I am one who believes, without reservation, that the Book of Mormon is our most powerful resource in missionary work, and that we need to rely on it more than we do (see *Preach My Gospel*, 104; Joseph B. Wirthlin, "The Book of Mormon: The Heart of Missionary Proselyting," *Ensign*, September 2002, 12). In fact, I believe that missionary work can largely be reduced to the simple act of inviting others to read the Book of Mormon, and their initial conversion can largely be reduced to the simple act of reading and praying about it. As Elder Joseph B. Wirthlin expressed, "If you want to reach people, if you want to change hearts, if you want to be successful in your missionary work, testify of the divinity of the Book of Mormon" ("The Book of Mormon: The Heart of Missionary Proselyting," 14). We need to let the Book of Mormon do the work in missionary work!

One missionary who understood this principle was Samuel H. Smith, brother of the Prophet Joseph and the first missionary of the restored Church.

> When Samuel left on his first mission, shortly following the organization of the Church, he was armed with a testimony of the truth and little else. But he needed little else. He had a testimony, and he had copies of the Book of Mormon—the missionary tool for conversion. He carried a knapsack with him that he filled with as many copies of this book as he could carry. He probably even carried one in his hand.
>
> You have to remember that this had never been done before. He didn't have a companion to show him how to use the Book of Mormon. There was no missionary training center for this young man. . . .
>
> [Two copies of the Book of Mormon that Samuel Smith placed] eventually were the means of converting a whole neighborhood, including Brigham Young and his family and Heber C. Kimball and his family. (Joseph B. Wirthlin, "The Book of Mormon: The Heart of Missionary Proselyting," 16)

As this story illustrates, there is a converting power in the Book of Mormon, and the more we rely on that power in missionary work, the more successful we will be. In fact, when we come to understand this principle, we realize that one reason why we teach a second, third, and fourth missionary lesson is simply to give us a reason and an excuse to return to the homes of our investigators *to find out if they have been reading the Book of Mormon*. This is exactly what Elder Bruce R. McConkie taught a group of missionaries in Okinawa, Japan, before concluding that "the [missionary] discussions are . . . a vehicle to get people to read the Book of Mormon! Conversion grows out of the Book of Mormon. . . . What we are interested in is getting people to read the Book of Mormon" (October 29, 1970; recording in author's possession).

This is why, as Elder Jeffrey R. Holland explained, "the first thing you will do when an investigator tells you he or she [has] not read and prayed about the Book of Mormon is *be devastated*!" (as quoted in *Preach My Gospel*, 8)

The Keystone of Our Religion

As long as I can remember, I have heard about the importance of giving away a copy of the Book of Mormon in missionary work. During the years that Ezra Taft Benson was the president of the Church, there was no message more often repeated than that we should flood the earth with the Book of Mormon. This must have been instilled in me very well—and at an early age—because one year, deducing from his pipe smoking that he was not a member of the Church, my brother and I left Santa Claus a Book of Mormon along with the traditional cookies and milk!

Though I understood that was what I *should* do, like so many members of the Church, I didn't yet understand *why*. Why do we invite others to read the book? What is the role of the Book of Mormon in our religion and why is it so important to missionary work?

The importance of the Book of Mormon in our religion is sometimes more obvious to those outside of the Church than within. Those not of our faith recognized the Book of Mormon as being so central and so distinctive to our Church that they nicknamed us "Mormons." Unfortunately, we may become so familiar with this book of scripture that we lose sight of how uniquely important it is to our church. The place of the Book of Mormon in our religion was best explained by the

Prophet Joseph Smith when he made these classic declarations: "Take away the Book of Mormon and the revelations and where is our religion? We have none" (Joseph F. Smith, *Teachings of the Prophet Joseph Smith* [Salt Lake City: Deseret Book, 1977], 71; see also Preach My Gospel, 103). On another occasion, he explained, "I told the Brethren that the Book of Mormon was the most correct of any book on earth, and *the keystone of our religion*, and a man would get nearer to God by abiding by its precepts, than by any other book" (see the introduction of the Book of Mormon; emphasis added).

"A keystone," President Ezra Taft Benson explained, "is the central stone in an arch. It holds all the other stones in place" ("The Book of Mormon—Keystone of Our Religion," *Ensign*, November 1986, 5). The dictionary defines keystone simply as "something on which associated things depend" (Random House Webster's College Dictionary, second definition). Thus, as the keystone of our religion, all that we believe *depends* on the Book of Mormon.

How our beliefs are dependent on the Book of Mormon was explained by President Ezra Taft Benson when he described three ways in which the Book of Mormon is the keystone of our religion. The Book of Mormon is the keystone in our witness of Christ, the keystone of our doctrine, and the keystone of testimony ("The Book of Mormon—Keystone of Our Religion," 5–7; see also *Preach My Gospel*, 104).

The Keystone in Our Witness of Christ

The Book of Mormon is the keystone in our witness of Christ because, as the subtitle declares, it is another testament of Jesus Christ.

> Unlike the Bible, which passed through generations of copyists, translators, and corrupt religionists who tampered with the text, the Book of Mormon came from writer to reader in just one inspired step of translation. Therefore, its testimony of the Master is clear, undiluted, and full of power. But it does even more. Much of the Christian world today rejects the divinity of the Savior. They question His miraculous birth, His perfect life, and the reality of His glorious resurrection. The Book of Mormon teaches in plain and unmistakable terms about the truth of all of those. It also provides the most complete explanation of the doctrine of the Atonement. Truly, this divinely inspired book is a keystone in bearing witness to the world that Jesus is the Christ. ("The Book of Mormon—Keystone of Our Religion," 5)

In the New Testament, special witnesses were invited to touch the resurrected body of Christ. In our day, special witnesses were invited to touch the gold plates. Interestingly, the result of each experience was basically the same: it was to made them special, physical witnesses of Jesus Christ. The message this conveys is simple yet profound. Though we are grateful for the witnesses of Christ found in the Bible, we do not have to depend solely on the witnesses of the past. Our testimony of Christ today depends primarily on the Book of Mormon. That is the book the Lord revealed in our day as another testament of Jesus Christ to renew faith in the Savior. That is the book the Lord prepared to confirm in our day the witness of the Bible regarding Jesus Christ. In short, the Book of Mormon is the book God sent to reveal Jesus Christ to mankind today and "a man [or woman] will get nearer to [Christ] by abiding by its precepts, than by any other book" (Joseph Smith, as quoted in the introduction of The Book of Mormon).

The Keystone of Our Doctrine

The Book of Mormon is also the keystone of our doctrine and teachings because it contains the "fulness of the gospel of Jesus Christ" (D&C 20:9). As President Ezra Taft Benson explained, "That does not mean it contains every teaching, every doctrine ever revealed. Rather, it means that in the Book of Mormon we will find the fulness of those doctrines required for our salvation. And they are taught plainly and simply so that even children can learn" ("The Book of Mormon—Keystone of Our Religion," 6). In other words, what it means that the Book of Mormon contains the "fulness of the gospel," is that it contains *all the basics*. There are many additional truths revealed in the Doctrine and Covenants and the Pearl of Great Price, but the Book of Mormon lays the foundation for these later revelations by teaching all the basic and fundamental principles of the gospel of Jesus Christ. Because those basic teachings are taught in such purity and power, the Prophet Joseph declared that the Book of Mormon is "the most correct of any book on earth" (see the introduction of the Book of Mormon), meaning that it is more doctrinally correct than any book, including the Bible. As a result, our knowledge of the gospel of Jesus Christ depends on the Book of Mormon.

As the primary source of our gospel knowledge, the Book of Mormon is the gospel rock or doctrinal foundation that the Church is built on today. The Lord explained to Nephi that when the Book of Mormon would come forth in the latter days, in it "shall be written my gospel . . . and my rock" (1 Nephi 13:36). Similarly, Oliver Cowdery was reminded of the "many instances" that the Spirit had confirmed to him that what he had written (as the chief scribe of the Book of Mormon) was true, and that he and Joseph were to "rely upon [the Book of Mormon]" in organizing the Church, "*for in them* [meaning in the words found in the Book of Mormon] *are all things written concerning the foundation of my church, my gospel, and my rock*" (D&C 18:2–4; emphasis added). Thus the Book of Mormon is the doctrinal foundation of the Church. It is the rock of gospel teachings that the Church is built on in our day. As President Ezra Taft Benson declared, we are "built on the rock of Christ *through* the Book of Mormon" ("The Book of Mormon—Keystone of Our Religion," 65; emphasis added). This is one reason why the Church could not be organized until *after* the Book of Mormon was published.

The Keystone of Testimony

In addition to being the keystone in our witness of Christ and our keystone of doctrine, the Book of Mormon is also the "keystone of testimony" ("The Book of Mormon—Keystone of Our Religion," 6). President Benson explained that "just as the arch crumbles if the keystone is removed, *so does all the Church stand or fall with the truthfulness of the Book of Mormon*. . . . If it can be discredited, the Prophet Joseph Smith goes with it. So does our claim to priesthood keys, and revelation, and the restored church. But in like manner, if the Book of Mormon be true—and millions have now testified that they have the witness of the Spirit that it is indeed true—*then one must accept the claims of the Restoration and all that accompanies it*" ("The Book of Mormon—Keystone of Our Religion," 6; emphasis added). The reasoning of President Benson on this point is powerful. Because it is the keystone of our religion, if the Book of Mormon is true, then it proves everything else about our religion is true by association. As a result, our testimonies, and the testimonies of our investigators, depend on the Book of Mormon.

One reason for this dramatic conclusion is that, as Christ explained, the truth of any work is known by its fruits (see Matthew 7:16–20; 3 Nephi 14:16–20). If the fruit is good, then the tree must be good. And because the Book of Mormon is the primary fruit of Joseph Smith and the Restoration, it becomes the primary evidence that our message is true—the proof that the gospel of Jesus Christ has been restored through the Prophet Joseph Smith (see *Preach My Gospel*, 103). As Elder Bruce R. McConkie explained, "If the Book of Mormon is true—then [it] . . . proves the truth of this great latter-day work" ("What Think Ye of the Book of Mormon?" *Ensign*, November 1983, 72).

One of my missionary companions, Elder Trochez, would often draw upon this principle to invite people to read the Book of Mormon. After we had taught the First Vision and testified of the Restoration, he would pose this situation: "If I had a cake, and I told you it was delicious—the *best* cake in the world—what would be the simplest, easiest way for you to find out if I were telling you the truth?" The investigator would invariably respond, "I would need to taste it." Then Elder Trochez would reach into his bag, pull out a copy of the Book of Mormon, and say, "This is your opportunity to 'taste it.' Read this book, and you can find out for yourself that everything we are telling you is true." As President Gordon B. Hinckley explained, "It is a tangible thing that can be handled, that can be read, that can be tested" ("The Great Things Which God Has Revealed," 82).

This concept of proving the truth of our message with the Book of Mormon must be clearly understood by missionaries because it is the reason why "*the Book of Mormon, combined with the Spirit, is [our] most powerful resource in missionary work*" (*Preach My Gospel*, 104; emphasis added) and "the greatest single tool which God has given us to convert the world" (Ezra Taft Benson, "A New Witness for Christ," *Ensign*, November 1984, 7). We cannot afford to underestimate the power and importance of this "small and simple thing" (Alma 37:6). The Book of Mormon is nothing less than the instrument that God has designed to allow people to "test" the truth of our message and gain a testimony for themselves. It is the God-given proof, the "convincing evidence," that our Church is true (L. Tom Perry, "'Bring Souls unto Me,'" *Ensign*, May 2009, 111). That is why "an essential part of conversion is receiving a witness from the Holy Ghost that the Book of Mormon is true" (*Preach My Gospel*, 103), because if our investigators can just come to know that its true, then they will know automatically that everything else we have taught them is true. And what is so exciting about all of this is that *everyone* can know that the Book of Mormon is true!

Gaining a Testimony of the Book of Mormon

The Book of Mormon begins and ends with a promise. In the introduction of the Book of Mormon and in the final chapter, we are given a simple formula, which, if followed, guarantees us a testimony of the Book of Mormon. It consists of three basic steps that always and without exception lead to a spiritual confirmation that the book is true: "We invite all men everywhere to *read* the Book of Mormon, to *ponder* in their hearts the message it contains, and then to *ask God*, the Eternal Father, in the name of Christ if the book is true. Those who pursue this course and ask in faith will gain a testimony of its truth and divinity by the power of the Holy Ghost" (see the introduction of the Book of Mormon; see also Moroni 10:3–5).

This is the universal promise from our Eternal Father. If we sincerely read, ponder, and pray in faith, then we are assured a testimony of the Book of Mormon. This promised testimony will not come by dramatic signs or archeological evidence, but by the power of the Holy Ghost. As Elder M. Russell Ballard reminded one protestant minister who requested to see the gold plates, "You could hold the Gold Plates in your hands, and you would not know any more about whether the Church is true than before." The way we gain a testimony, Elder Ballard concluded, is by reading the Book of Mormon and having the Spirit confirm it by feelings of conviction (*Our Search for Happiness* [Salt Lake City: Deseret Book, 2001], 24–25; see also Ballard transcript, *Mormon Newsroom*, October 2, 2007). Often that testimony will come gradually, a page at a time.

Inviting others to follow this process and gain that spiritual witness is the essence of missionary work, because once a person has obtained that testimony of the Book of Mormon, they will know by implication that everything else about our religion is true also. Specifically, the introduction lists three truths that our investigators will know automatically when they come to know that the Book of Mormon is true. It states, "Those who gain this divine witness from the Holy Spirit will also come to know by the same power that Jesus Christ is the Savior of the world, that Joseph Smith is his revelator and prophet in these last days, and that The Church of Jesus Christ of Latter-day Saints is the Lord's kingdom once again established on the earth, preparatory to the second coming of the Messiah" (see the introduction of the Book of Mormon).

If the Book of Mormon is true, then, of necessity, Jesus Christ is the Savior. This is because the Book of Mormon is another testament of Jesus Christ, and as such, it bears repeated testimony of the Savior. On average, "over one-half of all the verses in the Book of Mormon refer to our Lord" (Ezra Taft Benson, *A Witness and a Warning* [Salt Lake City: Deseret Book, 2009], 53). Not only does this confirm the testimony of Christ found in the Bible, but this new and additional testament provides us with an independent, modern witness of Christ. A testimony of Christ in our day must be based on the revelations of Christ given in our day, if it is to lead to salvation. This is true for us and our converts. We know Jesus Christ is the Savior when we know the Book of Mormon is true.

If the Book of Mormon is true, then Joseph Smith is a prophet. As mentioned earlier, in teaching his disciples how to discern true prophets from false, the Lord counseled, "Ye shall know them by their fruits" (Matthew 7:16). Just as good fruit does not come from a bad tree, so a true book does not come from a false prophet. If the Book of Mormon is true, then it follows automatically that Joseph Smith was a true prophet and that he translated the book by the gift and power of God. We know Joseph Smith is a prophet when we know the Book of Mormon is true.

If the Book of Mormon is true, then The Church of Jesus Christ of Latter-day Saints is the Lord's kingdom, once again established on the earth. This Church is built on the foundation of what is revealed in and through the Book of Mormon (see D&C 18:2–4). It is the keystone of our religion. If the book is true, then obviously the Church that rests upon it is too. We know this Church is true when we know the Book of Mormon is true.

As illustrated by these three examples, to gain a testimony of the Book of Mormon is to know automatically and implicitly that other things about our religion are true as well. While the three listed in the introduction are certainly among the most important, they are not the only truths that the Book of Mormon proves. For example, in the Doctrine and Covenants we read that the Book of Mormon *proves* "that the holy scriptures are true" (D&C 20:11), meaning that the Book of Mormon confirms the teachings of the Bible and therefore proves the Bible is true. In addition, the same verse declares that the Book of Mormon proves that "God does inspire men and call them to his holy work" in our day (D&C 20:11), meaning that the Book of Mormon proves that God still calls prophets today because He called Joseph Smith to translate the book. Finally, the Book of Mormon proves God "is the same God yesterday, today, and forever" (D&C 20:12), meaning that God has not changed but continues to be a God who speaks by revelation and performs miracles in our day, just as He did through the coming forth of the Book of Mormon. The verse summary of Doctrine and Covenants 20 states that all of this means that "the Book of Mormon proves the divinity of the latter-day work."

But the Book of Mormon does even more. Because it is the keystone of our religion, it is the proof and reason for all that we believe, even the very existence of God. Referring specifically to the Book of Mormon, the inspired founding document of the Church declares, "By these things we know that there is a God in heaven" (D&C 20:17). This is a powerful concept. Because our religion is *restored* religion, we do not have to rely exclusively on the revelations of the past to know God exists. Our belief in God is based on what He has revealed and restored in our day. We know there is a God in heaven because we know the Book of Mormon is true and has come forth by the power of God in the latter-days.

And that's not all! This revelation continues to explain that because of the Book of Mormon, we know that God created man in His own image, that by transgression to God's laws mankind is in a fallen state; that God gave His Only Begotten Son to suffer, die, and be resurrected from the dead to save us; and that all who believe in Christ, are baptized, and endure to the end will be saved (see D&C 20:17–25). The point of this declaration is not only to summarize our basic beliefs, but also to show that the truths of the plan of salvation and gospel of Jesus Christ are confirmed by, and restored to us through, the Book of Mormon. Therefore, "By these things [found in the Book of Mormon] we know" that the plan of salvation and gospel of Christ are true (D&C 20:17–25). (Incidentally, that is why *Preach My Gospel* has missionaries teach the plan of salvation and the gospel of Jesus Christ as lessons two and three, after they have taught the Restoration.)

This is how the Book of Mormon proves, sustains, and upholds all things connected with our religion. Can we see now what a pivotal place the Book of Mormon has in missionary work? It is the keystone of our religion, the foundation of all that we believe about Christ and His gospel in these latter days; it is the primary means by which these things were revealed and restored. As a result, it is the keystone in our testimony. If it is true, then everything else about our Church is true by association. This makes the Book of Mormon the divine evidence of all that we believe. It is the proof God offers the world to test if His latter-day work is true.

As latter-day prophets and apostles have declared,

> The truthfulness of the Book of Mormon—its origins, its doctrines, and the circumstances of its coming forth—is central to the truthfulness of The Church of Jesus Christ of Latter-day Saints. The integrity of this church and more than 165 years of its restoration experience stand or fall with the veracity or falsity of the Book of Mormon. (Jeffrey R. Holland, *Christ and the New Covenant*, 345)

> Either the Book of Mormon is true, or it is false. . . . It either came from heaven or from hell. And it is time for all those who seek salvation to find out for themselves. (Bruce R. McConkie, "What Think Ye of the Book of Mormon?" 73)

> We do not have to prove the Book of Mormon is true. The book is its own proof. All we need to do is read it and declare it! The Book of Mormon is not on trial—[we are]. (Ezra Taft Benson, "A New Witness of Christ," 13)

> Do eternal consequences rest upon our response to this book? Yes, either to our blessing or our condemnation. (Ezra Taft Benson, "The Book of Mormon—Keystone of Our Religion," 7)

The plain fact is that salvation itself is at stake in this matter. If the Book of Mormon is true . . . then to accept it and believe its doctrines is to be saved, and to reject it and walk contrary to its teachings is to be damned.

Let this message be sounded in every ear with an angelic trump; let it roll round the earth in resounding claps of never-ending thunder; let it be whispered in every heart by the still, small voice. Those who believe the Book of Mormon and accept Joseph Smith as a prophet thereby open the door to salvation [by Christ]. . . . It is the book that will save the world. (Bruce R. McConkie, "What Think Ye of the Book of Mormon?" 74)

The Lord Himself has stated, "Those who receive [the Book of Mormon] in faith, and work righteousness, shall receive a crown of eternal life; but those who harden their hearts in unbelief, and reject it, it shall turn to their own condemnation" (D&C 20:14–15).

4

ANSWERING QUESTIONS WITH THE FIRST VISION AND THE BOOK OF MORMON

Why do "**Mormons**" not drink coffee?
Why did "Mormons" once practice plural marriage?
Why do "Mormons" pay tithing?
Why do "Mormons" worship on Sunday?
Why do "Mormons" practice baptisms for the dead?

As members and as missionaries, we receive all kinds of questions. These are just a few of some of the more common ones that might come up in a conversation about the Church. So how do we respond? Take a moment to consider how you would answer each of the questions above.

Up to this point, we have learned some important principles in sharing the gospel; for example, we have learned why *Preach My Gospel* counsels us to start at the beginning by laying a foundation of the Restoration. In doing so, we have discovered that "there is no better place to start such a discussion than with the First Vision" (Boyd K. Packer, "The Only True Church," 80). And as a result, we should take the quickest and most direct route to the Sacred Grove. Having done that, we are to follow up with an invitation to read the Book of Mormon, the keystone of our religion, which "proves the divinity of the latter-day work" (D&C 20 verse summary). Simply stated, the First Vision is our message and the Book of Mormon is the proof.

But all of this is theoretical. The real test of how well we have understood these principles is found in how well we apply them. How well did we implement these ideas in answering questions listed previously? How can we answer questions about our faith in a way that introduces the Restoration, shares the First Vision, and invites others to read the Book of Mormon?

Sometimes I like to put my seminary students on the spot and invite them to answer some of these questions. Typically, they try to come up with some justification for our practices as they stumble through a response. I surprise them when I announce that we can answer all of these questions with one single response. That gets their attention. Then I give the answer:

A. Because of a revelation given to Joseph Smith.

Think about that for a moment. That simple answer responds to each of the questions perfectly. We don't drink coffee because of a revelation known as the Word of Wisdom, found in Doctrine and Covenants 89. We practiced plural marriage in the past because of a revelation recorded in Doctrine and Covenants 132 and ended that practice because of a revelation recorded in Official Declaration 1. We pay tithing because of a revelation recorded in Doctrine and Covenants119. We worship on Sunday because that was the day identified as "the Lord's day" in a revelation given on Sunday and recorded in Doctrine and Covenants 59. Instructions for the practice of baptisms for the dead are recorded in Doctrine and Covenants 124, 127, and 128. And so on.

In fact, all of our differences as a church are the result of revelation. We do all that we do because God commanded us to through latter-day revelation given to living prophets, primarily Joseph Smith. Consider that as you look again at the questions at the start of the chapter. Although we could try to justify each of these practices; for example, coffee has addictive substances, the Israelites in the Old Testament practiced plural marriage and paid tithing, and the Saints in the New Testament worshipped on Sunday. But ultimately, we have practiced these things because we were directed to practice them by revelation through modern prophets.

I believe there is power in recognizing and emphasizing that. All that sets us apart as a church, all that makes us different and true, can be summarized in a single word: *revelation*. As a result, almost all questions about our faith can be answered the same way—because of a revelation, typically one given to Joseph Smith.

Not only is that answer true, but it is also a great missionary response. By responding in this way, we immediately begin to introduce the concept of a restoration and all that goes with it, including modern revelation and living prophets. It also introduces them to the name of Joseph Smith, which they may have never heard of. As a result, it will often lead the honest in heart to ask another question, an even better question. With any curiosity, their next question might be:

Q. Who is Joseph Smith?

If you ever have the privilege of being asked this question, it will be hard to contain yourself from exclaiming, "I'm so glad you asked!" This beautiful question allows you to take the quickest and most direct route to the Sacred Grove. It is a perfect opportunity to teach and testify with all the energy of your soul of the First Vision.

A. Teach and testify of the First Vision.

Teaching the First Vision will quickly help you identify the honest in heart and the sincere truth seekers. They will be the ones who thoughtfully consider that, if what you have just shared is true, it is the single most important event in the history of Christianity since Jesus Christ was resurrected. They will be the ones who either verbally or in their hearts ask:

Q. How can I know for myself that what you have told me is true?

By now, the answer to this question should be obvious to us. God has given us proof, divine evidence, the fruits by which we can test if this great latter-day work is true. And so our answer is:

A. Read the Book of Mormon and pray about it.

The Book of Mormon is the keystone of our religion. It is the proof of our whole message, the divine evidence that there has been a restoration. As a result, we are to use the Book of Mormon in answering questions about the Church. As President Ezra Taft Benson explained,

> All objections, whether they be on abortion, plural marriage, seventh-day worship, etc., basically hinge on whether Joseph Smith and his successors were and are prophets of God receiving divine revelation. . . .

Therefore, the only problem the objector has to resolve for himself is whether the Book of Mormon is true. For if the Book of Mormon is true, then Jesus is the Christ, Joseph Smith was his prophet, The Church of Jesus Christ of Latter-day Saints is true, and it is being led today by a prophet receiving revelation. Our main task is to declare the gospel and do it effectively. We are not obligated to answer every objection. Every man eventually is backed up to the wall of faith, and there he must make his stand. (*A Witness and a Warning*, 4–5; see also *Preach My Gospel*, 109)

Answering with the First Vision and the Book of Mormon

Though our own informal missionary conversations may not go *quite* as smoothly as outlined above, this provides a pattern for answering questions about our faith that will help us more fully use the First Vision and the Book of Mormon in sharing the gospel. A real-life example of this pattern in action is provided by Elder Dale G. Renlund, who shared this beautiful experience:

> My wife and I once visited a university in Athens, Greece. As part of that visit, we were taken on a sightseeing tour. While we were actually inside the Parthenon, our hostess, a graduate student in archaeology, said, "Next, I would like to take you to my favorite coffee house in all of Athens."
>
> My wife said that we would love to go with her, but she said, "Please don't be offended if we don't drink the coffee."
>
> Our hostess asked, "You don't drink coffee?"
>
> "No," we answered.
>
> "Why not?" she asked.
>
> As I was formulating a response, my wife said, "The short answer is this: In 1820, a young man by the name of Joseph Smith went into a grove in upstate New York to pray. He wanted to know which church he should join. There he saw God, our Heavenly Father, and His Son, Jesus Christ. Joseph was told he should join none of the churches. But he was told that through him, the Church Jesus had established while He was on the earth would be restored. The restoration would be through a process of revelation. And it is through revelation that we know that we shouldn't drink coffee. My husband will now explain it to you further."

How do we really explain ourselves? How do we explain anything that we do or believe if we do not go back to the Sacred Grove and establish the principle of revelation, that God reveals His will to prophets in this day and age? We obey because we have understood through the Holy Ghost something of eternal import. The reason you and I observe the Word of Wisdom, obey the law of chastity, and keep other commandments is because of revelation. (Dale G. Renlund, Facebook post, March 1, 2016)

As this story powerfully illustrates, all questions about our Church really come down to the principle of modern revelation that is perfectly established by sharing the First Vision.

Another real-life example of this pattern in action is provided by Elder M. Russell Ballard, who showed how the Book of Mormon can be used in answering questions and handling objections to the Church. As a former mission president, he explained,

One of my missionaries came to me some time ago. He was a fine missionary. I asked him, "Elder, how can I help you?"

"President," he said, "I think I'm losing my testimony."

I couldn't believe it. I asked him how that could be possible.

"For the first time I have read some anti-Mormon literature," he said. "I have some questions, and nobody will answer them for me. I am confused, and I think I am losing my testimony."

I asked him what his questions were, and he told me. They were the standard anti-Church issues, but I wanted a little time to gather materials so I could provide meaningful answers. So we set up an appointment ten days later, at which time I told him I would answer everyone of his questions. As he started to leave, I stopped him.

"Elder, you've asked me several questions here today," I said. "Now I have one for you."

"Yes, President?"

"How long has it been since you read from the Book of Mormon?" I asked.

His eyes dropped. He looked at the floor for a while. Then he looked at me. "It's been a long time, President," he confessed.

"All right," I said. "You have given me my assignment. It's only fair that I give you yours. I want you to promise me that you will read in the Book of Mormon for at least one hour every day between now and our next appointment." He agreed that he would do that.

Ten days later he returned to my office, and I was ready. I pulled out my papers to start answering his questions. But he stopped me.

"President," he said, "that isn't going to be necessary." Then he explained, "I know that the Book of Mormon is true. I know Joseph Smith is a prophet of God."

"Well, that's great," I said, "but you're going to get answers to your questions anyway. I worked a long time on this, so you just sit there and listen." (M. Russell Ballard, "'When Shall These Things Be?'" *Ensign*, December 1996, 56–61)

As this story shows, the real question people need to find the answer to is whether the Book of Mormon is true. When they know the answer to that, it has a way of answering all their other questions. Consequently, if people will just read, ponder, and pray about the Book of Mormon, they will come to know that it is true. And once they know that it is true, they will know automatically that the First Vision really happened, that Joseph Smith is a true prophet, that he received revelation, and that because of those revelations we don't drink coffee, we pay tithing, we worship on Sunday, and do all the things we do and ever did as a church.

That is how we can answer all questions about our faith with the First Vision and the Book of Mormon. All of our differences as a church can be summarized in a single word—revelation. And what better way to introduce others to latter-day revelation than with the First Vision and the Book of Mormon? Interestingly, this is how the Lord always intended that they be used. In fact, they were designed to be the chief resources in latter-day missionary work, and this was known and prophesied of from the beginning of the world.

Righteousness from Heaven and Truth from the Earth

Over five thousand years ago, Enoch was shown a panoramic vision of the history and destiny of the earth. As part of this vision, he saw the latter days and the wickedness and destruction that would precede the Second Coming of the Lord Jesus Christ. Fortunately, this gloom and despair was contrasted with a message of hope and salvation. He was promised that the Lord's people would be saved (see Moses 7:60–61). Then, as an explanation of how that salvation would be made available, the Lord assured Enoch that "righteousness will I send down out of heaven; and truth will I send forth out of the earth" (Moses 7:62).

Righteousness from heaven and truth from the earth. That would be the means by which salvation would be offered in the last days. But what exactly was the Lord describing to Enoch? When has righteousness come down out of heaven and when has truth ever come from the earth?

President Ezra Taft Benson answered these questions when he declared, "We have seen the marvelous fulfillment of that prophecy in our generation. The Book of Mormon has come forth out of the earth, filled with truth . . . [and] God has also sent down righteousness from heaven. The Father himself appeared with His Son to the Prophet Joseph Smith" ("The Gift of Modern Revelation," *Ensign*, November 1986, 79–80). According to President Benson, this verse has specific reference to the First Vision and the Book of Mormon. What better way to describe that glorious appearance of the Father and the Son (and other angelic messengers) than "righteousness" from heaven? And what a perfect description of the Book of Mormon, which was buried in the Hill Cumorah, and literally came forth as "truth" from the earth.

Not only did Enoch learn of the First Vision and the Book of Mormon, but he was shown their purpose in missionary work. These two latter-day miracles would be used as the primary resources in missionary work to "bear testimony of [the] Only Begotten" Son, Jesus Christ (Moses 7:62). Not only do they confirm the truths of Christ found in the Bible, but these latter-day witnesses of Christ, testify that He lives and speaks today. They provide another testament of Jesus Christ and are the chief revelations in the Restoration of His gospel.

"And righteousness and truth will I cause to sweep the earth as with a flood" (Moses 7:62). That is Enoch's prophecy of how the First Vision and the Book of Mormon will be used in missionary work. They will "sweep the earth as with a flood" as missionaries use them to teach and testify to all the world that Jesus Christ lives and speaks today, and His gospel has been restored. We fulfill this prophecy every time missionaries faithfully teach lesson one of *Preach My Gospel*. Our commission is to flood the earth with that message. "We have a great work to perform in a very short time. We must flood the earth with the Book of Mormon" (Ezra Taft Benson, "Flooding the Earth with the Book of Mormon," *Ensign*, November 1988, 5).

And when we do, what can we expect will happen? Enoch was shown that as we rely on these two great missionary resources, we will "gather out [the Lord's] elect from the four quarters of the earth" (Moses

7:62). That is one of the great secrets of missionary work—missionaries who rely on the First Vision and the Book of Mormon to testify of Christ and His restored gospel have more success in gathering the elect. The elect respond to this message, and it is the elect that we are sent to find and gather. So while this bold message may repel some, it will also attract the ones we are searching for. The honest in heart will feel the Spirit, recognize the truth, and gather to His Church. "My sheep hear my voice, . . . " the Lord explained, "and they follow me" (John 10:27).

As we have now seen, the First Vision and the Book of Mormon are two of the greatest resources ever given in missionary work. They are the foundation of faith and the keys to conversion in the latter days. Joseph Smith relied on them in his missionary efforts, and we still follow that example today. They are taught in lesson one of *Preach My Gospel*, and they have been a part of the first missionary discussions for generations. They have led millions—and will lead *billions*—to the true Christ and His true Church. And it was known from the beginning of time that this would be their purpose and destiny.

If we are to help save the Lord's people in the last days, if we are to bear powerful testimony of Jesus Christ, if we are to gather out the elect from the four quarters of the earth, if we are to be the missionaries the Lord expects and the missionaries the world needs, then we must rely on the First Vision and the Book of Mormon to teach and testify that the gospel has been restored and that Jesus Christ lives and speaks to mankind today. May we continue with even greater determination to flood the earth with the First Vision and the Book of Mormon—righteousness from heaven and truth from the earth.

5

THE ONLY TRUE CHURCH

As important as the First Vision and the Book of Mormon are, they are not the end of our journey, but only the beginning. What led Joseph Smith into the Sacred Grove was the desire to find the true Church of Jesus Christ so that he could be saved. But he didn't actually find the true Church in the First Vision, only the promise that it would soon be restored (see *History of the Church*, 4:536). Nor did he find it in the Book of Mormon. There he simply uncovered the doctrinal foundation of what the true Church would believe. But visions and books do not authorize one to form a church or perform an ordinance, and so his search was not yet over. He still needed to find the true Church of Jesus Christ.

The next big step in that journey came while translating the Book of Mormon, specifically "the account given of the Savior's ministry to the [Nephites]" (Oliver Cowdery's account, in the JS—H Appendix). Those familiar with this account will remember that the first thing that Christ did after inviting the Nephites to "feel the prints of the nails in his hands and in his feet" (3 Nephi 11:15) was to call twelve disciples and give them "power to baptize" (3 Nephi 11:22). The Lord then warned the multitude that only those who are baptized can be saved (see 3 Nephi 11:33–34).

While translating these verses, Joseph Smith and Oliver Cowdery realized that they needed to be baptized and that, problematically, "none had [priesthood] authority from God to administer the ordinances of the Gospel" (Oliver Cowdery's account, in the JS—H Appendix). As a result, Joseph and Oliver "went into the woods to pray and inquire of the Lord" on the subject (JS—H 1:68).

The Prophet Joseph Smith described what happened next in these words,

> While we were thus employed, praying and calling upon the Lord, a messenger from heaven descended in a cloud of light, and having laid his hands upon us, he ordained us, saying:
>
> Upon you my fellow servants, in the name of Messiah, I confer the Priesthood of Aaron, which holds the keys of the ministering of angels, and of the gospel of repentance, and of baptism by immersion for the remission of sins; and this shall never be taken again from the earth until the sons of Levi do offer again an offering unto the Lord in righteousness. (JS—H 1:68–69)

This heavenly messenger identified himself as John the Baptist (JS—H 1:72). There is so much that could be said about these verses, but to missionaries, this means one thing in particular: "the authority to perform the ordinance of baptism" (*Preach My Gospel*, 37) has been restored. And who better to restore that authority than John the Baptist, the same man who baptized the Lord Himself? Think of the power of this claim! John the Baptist gave us the priesthood authority to baptize. Every Bible-believing Christian should want to know this. Teaching this event prepares the way for us to invite our investigators and friends to be "baptized by someone holding the priesthood authority of God" (*Preach My Gospel*, 40).

But what about the Church? Does the authority to baptize authorize us to organize the true Church? On this same occasion, John the Baptist explained to the Prophet Joseph "that he acted under the direction of Peter, James and John, who held the keys of the Priesthood of Melchizedek, which Priesthood, he said, would in due time be conferred on us, and that I should be called the first Elder of the Church" (JS—H 1:72).

Notice that: "The first Elder *of the Church*" (emphasis added). With the restoration of the Melchizedek Priesthood, Joseph Smith received the authority to lead and to "organize the Church of Jesus Christ again on the earth" (*Preach My Gospel*, 37). And again, who better to confer that authority than Peter, James, and John, the very apostles Jesus Christ Himself called to lead the Church after His Ascension into heaven? Think of it. New Testament apostles restored the priesthood authority to lead the Church of Jesus Christ today! What Bible-believing Christian wouldn't want to know this? Do we fully appreciate the power of our message?

With the restoration of the priesthood authority to organize the Church, Joseph Smith's journey to find the true Church of Jesus Christ was complete. Joseph Smith—History has now taken us full circle, and we end where we began. What first led Joseph Smith into the Sacred Grove "was to know which of all the sects was right, that [he] might know which to join" (JS—H 1:18). Now, with the priesthood, he was authorized to organize the true Church of Jesus Christ again on the earth. He had finally found what he was looking for, and in his journey, so have we. And so have our investigators. Our search is over—we have found the true Church, the only church authorized to administer salvation and offer the true path to heaven. The Church of Jesus Christ of Latter-day Saints was organized April 6, 1830, and teaching this provides the perfect opportunity to invite others to join the true Church of Jesus Christ.

The Doctrine of One True Church

"Inevitably (and properly) the 'true church' doctrine emerges very early in any serious discussion of the gospel" (Boyd K. Packer, "The Only True Church," 80). This is because it is the result of teaching the Restoration. When we follow the inspired pattern of Joseph Smith—History, as lesson one of *Preach My Gospel* trains us to do, we find ourselves emphasizing the First Vision, the Book of Mormon, and the restoration of the priesthood, which authorized Joseph Smith to organize the Church of Jesus Christ. As we do so, it is natural for those guided by the Spirit to declare the powerful, climactic conclusion that this is the one true Church of Jesus Christ.

In making that declaration, we ought to be aware that there will be some who are offended by that bold assertion. They believe that it is presumptuous to make the claim of being the only true Church and often label us as bigoted, narrow-minded, and even unchristian. In fact, there are two particular verses of scripture on this subject that seem to be a source of controversy. One is the announcement of the Lord that this is "the only true and living church upon the face of the whole earth" (D&C 1:30). The second is the contrasting point found in the Lord's instruction to Joseph Smith regarding other churches, that he "must join none of them, for they were all wrong" (JS—H 1:19). Because of the fundamental place of these two scriptural statements in our religion and how frequently they come up in missionary work, they need to be addressed and understood.

But before we begin to analyze them, there is one thing we need to understand clearly. These statements came from the Lord Jesus Christ. Because we are not the author of them, we do not have the right to edit them. They are the Lord's words, and we should not feel the need to avoid, excuse, or apologize for them. As missionaries, we need to understand these words and faithfully teach them to others. As a result, my effort here is to explain them, not explain them away. There is a big difference.

The True and Living Church

The first of these two statements is found in the Lord's preface to the Doctrine and Covenants, wherein He declared: "And also those to whom these commandments were given, might have power to lay the foundation of this church, and to bring it forth out of obscurity and out of darkness, *the only true and living church upon the face of the whole earth*, with which I, the Lord, am well pleased, speaking unto the church collectively and not individually" (D&C 1:30; emphasis added).

When properly taught in the context of the Restoration, it becomes clear what the Lord meant when He made this bold announcement. This is the *restored* Church of Jesus Christ. The Church Christ organized in the New Testament was lost through apostasy but has now been restored to the earth through the Prophet Joseph Smith.

To be the only true and living church requires at least four basic components that combine to form the foundation of the Church of

Jesus Christ in every dispensation. All four of these are found today in The Church of Jesus Christ of Latter-day Saints.

First, to be *true*, the Church must have *the truth*, meaning the fulness of the gospel. The fulness of gospel truth has always been part of the foundation of Christ's Church. The Lord explained to the Nephites that "if it be called in my name then it is my church, if it so be that they are built upon my gospel" (3 Nephi 27:8). And in our dispensation, He gave similar instruction, commanding us to "build up my church, upon the foundation of my gospel" (D&C 18:5). As used here, the gospel consists of the truths of salvation, or all the doctrines and principles we must believe and obey to be saved by Jesus Christ. Because gospel truths were lost through apostasy and restored through Joseph Smith, only this Church has the fulness of the gospel in plainness and purity. As a result, only this Church can claim to be the Lord's *true* Church.

But to be the true Church requires more than simply having the gospel truth. "True" is also variously defined as authentic, genuine, valid, or authorized, as opposed to an imitation or counterfeit. For example, a "true" or valid driver's license is one that is issued legally by someone *authorized* and *approved* by the government, as opposed to a fake or counterfeit created by someone who is not. Likewise, to be the true Church of Jesus Christ, a church must be authorized and approved *by* Jesus Christ. This authorization is granted to a church through the authority of the priesthood, which gives it the legal right to represent Jesus Christ and authoritatively bear His name. As we have seen, it was only after he had obtained priesthood authority that Joseph Smith was authorized to organize the Church. Without this authorization from Jesus Christ, a church cannot claim to be His true Church. Because the priesthood was lost during the apostasy and restored through Joseph Smith, only this Church has this authority from Jesus Christ. Therefore, as President Henry B. Eyring has taught, "this is the true Church, the only true Church, because in it are the keys of the priesthood" ("The True and Living Church," Eyring, *Ensign*, May 2008, 20).

In addition to being true, it is also the only *living* Church. What gives life to a church is revelation. If Christ does not actively speak to a church, it cannot claim to be His. Without that connection to the Living Christ, a church is dead. "I am the true vine," the Lord explained, and we as members of His Church "are the branches." If we cut ourselves off from Him, we wither and die (see John 15:1–6).

As President John Taylor taught, "We require a living tree—a living fountain—living intelligence, proceeding from the living priesthood in heaven, through the living priesthood on earth. . . . It always required new revelations, adapted to the peculiar circumstances in which the churches or individuals were placed. Adam's revelation did not instruct Noah to build his ark. . . . All [the former Saints] had revelations for themselves . . . and so must we" (Taylor, *Gospel Kingdom* [Salt Lake City: Bookcraft, 1987], 34). Since the Apostasy, no other Christian church I know of even believes such revelation is possible. Because only this Church receives direct revelation from the living Christ, it is His only true and *living* Church.

Related to the need for revelation, to be the *living* Church, it must be led by *living* prophets. Christ is always the head of His Church, but in His physical absence He leads and guides it through living prophets and apostles who receive direction from Him. This was Paul's point when he declared that the Church is always to be "built upon the foundation of the apostles and prophets, Jesus Christ himself being the chief corner stone" (Ephesians 2:20). It is also why, in the first revelation given to the newly restored Church, Jesus Christ proclaimed that Joseph Smith was a prophet and commanded the Saints to "give heed unto all his words . . . for his word ye shall receive, as if from mine own mouth" (D&C 21:4–5). Without living prophets and apostles to represent and receive revelation from Jesus Christ, a church cannot claim to be Christ's. The Great Apostasy began with the deaths of the apostles and ended when the Lord called Joseph Smith. Since that time, we have always had a *living* prophet receiving revelation from the *living* Christ, which makes this His true and *living* Church.

Thus, The Church of Jesus Christ of Latter-day Saints is the only *true* and *living* Church of Jesus Christ. These four components—gospel truth, priesthood authority, living prophets, and modern revelation— make up four foundational cornerstones of the true and living Church. They are what allow the Church to be built on the rock foundation of Jesus Christ (see Matthew 16:18).

The Only True Church

But perhaps the most controversial word in the verse is also the most important. It is the word *only*. This is the "*only* true and living church upon the face of the whole earth" (D&C 1:30; emphasis added).

As controversial as this doctrine may be to some, the doctrine of one true Church makes logical sense. How could two different churches, teaching conflicting doctrines, both be true? One plus one cannot be two and also three. All churches may be wrong (see JS—H 1:19), but only one can possibly be true (D&C 1:30). Because God is a God of order and not the author of confusion, it should be obvious that He will have only one true Church, not thousands of different competing and conflicting factions. As President Boyd K. Packer explained, "The doctrine [of one true Church] is true; it is logical. The opposite position is not" ("The Only True Church," 82).

The opposite position he is referring to is the currently popular claim that all churches are true and lead to heaven and that it therefore doesn't matter which one you belong to. I was first introduced to this deceptive idea on my mission when, after teaching the Restoration, I was told, "Of course your Church is true. They're all true." That response completely surprised me. It simply never occurred to me that someone could claim to accept that this Church was true and yet have no desire to join it. Nor was I ready for the apathy and disinterest that this all-churches-are-true idea creates.

But in this powerful verse, the Lord plainly states His views on the matter. This is the "only true and living church" (D&C 1:30). He does not say this is *a* true church or that all churches are true and ours is the *truest*. He said with unmistakable clarity that this is the *only* true Church. This is something the Lord does not budge on, and neither can we. "While this [idea of all churches being true] seems to be very generous, it just cannot be true. . . . Do [we] realize that the notion that all churches are equal presupposes that the *true* church of Jesus Christ actually does not exist anywhere?" (Boyd K. Packer, "The Only True Church," 82).

It is important to recognize that in saying that this is the "only true and living church," the Lord is referring to the *Church*, not individuals. He even specifically states that He is speaking "collectively and not individually" (D&C 1:30). This means that the Lord is speaking in general terms of the Church as an organization and its membership as a whole. He is not singling out and comparing individual members to those of other faiths. As a result, this does not mean that you will not find good people in other churches, even people who live as wholesome and upright of lives as Latter-day Saints. It means that a religious organization is either true or it is not. We are comparing churches, not individuals, when we make this assertion.

As President Packer reminded us, "We know there are decent, respectable, humble people in many churches, Christian and otherwise. In turn, sadly enough, there are so-called Latter-day Saints who by comparison are not as worthy, for they do not keep their covenants. But it is not a matter of comparing individuals. We are not baptized collectively, nor will we be judged collectively. Good conduct without the ordinances of the gospel will neither redeem nor exalt mankind; covenants and the ordinances are essential" ("The Only True Church," 82). This is exactly why good people from other faiths still need to find and join the only true and living Church.

Join None of Them, for They Are All Wrong

The second statement from the Lord on this subject that some find troubling is found in the Lord's response to Joseph Smith in the First Vision. After asking the Lord which church was true, Joseph Smith recalled, "I was answered that I must join none of them, for they were all wrong; and the Personage who addressed me said that all their creeds were an abomination in his sight; that those professors were all corrupt; that: 'they draw near to me with their lips, but their hearts are far from me, they teach for doctrines the commandments of men, having a form of godliness, but they deny the power thereof'" (JS—H 1:19).

The primary objection to this plain statement from the Lord is over the phrase *they were all wrong*, in describing other Christian churches. As harsh as this may sound to some, it is a fundamental position of our faith. If there had been no Apostasy to make all churches wrong, then there would be no need for a Restoration to provide one church that is right. The doctrine that "they [are] all wrong" because of apostasy is simply the inescapable and obvious counterpart to the previously discussed doctrine that, because of the Restoration, this is "the only true and living church" (D&C 1:30).

Those who take issue with this statement usually do so on the grounds of truth. "How can other churches be wrong," they argue, "if they have some truth?" Our response to this is simple. We freely acknowledge that other churches have truth. In fact, we openly encourage our investigators to keep all the truth they have. That is why "to people everywhere we simply say, 'You bring with you all the good that you have, and let us add to it'" (Gordon B. Hinckley, "Words of the Living Prophet," *Liahona*, June 1997, 32). Or, as Joseph Smith expressed it, "We don't ask any people to throw away any good they have got; we only ask them to come and get more" (*Teachings of the Prophet Joseph Smith*, 275). But having some truth is not enough to be the true Church.

In the courts of the United States, when a person is put under oath, they swear to tell the truth, the whole truth, and nothing but the truth. Anything more or less than this is considered a lie, even to the Lord (see D&C 93:25). Understanding this definition of truth and untruth helps us understand the meaning of the Lord's statement that "they were all wrong" (JS—H 1:19). One reason why they were all considered wrong is that none of these other churches had the whole truth, or the fulness of the gospel. Despite the partial truths that they had, "they [were], nonetheless, incomplete" (Boyd K. Packer, "The Only True and Living Church," *Ensign*, December 1971, 40). This is why there was a need for a restoration of the fulness of the gospel.

Not only do they not have the "whole truth," but none of these other churches has "nothing but the truth." In addition to the many truths they have, they have also inherited many uninspired ideas and philosophies of men that emerged during the Apostasy. These notions are now mingled with scripture and taught as if they were the word of God. These man-made and uninspired doctrines are what the Lord was referring to when he said that "all their creeds were an abomination in his sight . . . [and] they teach for doctrines the commandments of men"; because Joseph was to remain uninfluenced by these uninspired ideas that exist in other churches, the Lord counseled him to "join none of them" (JS—H 1:19).

Perhaps the best example of uninspired, man-made doctrine is found in the creeds of traditional Christianity, which define God as an incomprehensible and impersonal being without body, parts, or passions. This description of God is simply not inspired, at least not inspired by the Lord (see D&C 123:7). The First Vision instantly refuted this false concept of God by revealing the true God as being a loving, approachable, personal Father in Heaven, who is like man in form. It was specifically of these false descriptions of God that the Lord spoke when He pointedly declared that "their creeds were an abomination in his sight" (JS—H 1:19).

Because these other churches do not have the fulness of the gospel (the whole truth) and because they do not have the gospel in its purity (nothing but the truth), they cannot offer the true path to salvation in the celestial kingdom. While they can freely praise and worship God in their churches, they can never fully come unto Him and find salvation in His kingdom. Perhaps this is what the Lord was referring to when He said, "They draw near to me with their lips, but their hearts are far from me" (JS—H 1:19).

Some object to this by appealing to the fact that many members of other churches are sincere Christians, but *sincerity alone cannot lead to salvation.* We are commanded to worship the Lord "in sincerity *and in truth*" (Joshua 24:14; emphasis added), because without truth, our sincerity is in vain. For example, a woman can sincerely follow the directions of a map, but if it is a map of the wrong state, it will not lead her to where she wants to go. Likewise, there are many sincere believers out there who are not following the right path to heaven because they have been given the wrong map. One can worship in sincerity in any church, but because only in this church can we find the fulness of the gospel, it is only here that we can fully worship in sincerity *and* in truth. As for those sincere Christians of other churches, they will have the opportunity to demonstrate their sincerity when missionaries offer them *the truth.*

Our Uncompromising Position as the One True Church

The doctrine that this is "the only true and living church" and that all other churches are wrong, makes perfect sense in the context of the Restoration (D&C 1:30). But for those who do not understand or believe in a universal apostasy, this doctrine is sometimes inaccurately viewed as presumptuous and bigoted, and it sometimes stirs up controversy. As a result, there are some in the Church who seem to be a little embarrassed by these words from the Lord. They wonder if we should not avoid this doctrine altogether, or if we should no longer make the claim of being the only true Church of Jesus Christ.

> As President Boyd K. Packer reminded us, there are some who ask whether we should "make one accommodation and set this doctrine aside? Would it not be better to have more accept what would be left of the gospel than the relatively few who are converted now? . . .

Some have recommended that we confine ourselves strictly to evidences of the gospel: happy family life, and temperate living, and so on.

Could we not use the words better or best? The word only really isn't the most appealing way to begin a discussion of the gospel.

If we thought only in terms of diplomacy or popularity, surely we should change our course. ("The Only True Church," 81)

But when faced with these tempting arguments, President Packer declared us that "the position that The Church of Jesus Christ of Latter-day Saints is the only true church upon the face of the earth is fundamental. Perhaps it would be more convenient and palatable and popular if we were to avoid it; nevertheless, we are under a sacred obligation and a sacred trust to hold to it. It is not merely an admission; it is a positive declaration. It is so fundamental that we cannot yield on this point" ("The Only True and Living Church," 40; emphasis added).

We cannot yield on this point because to do so is to deny the mission and message of the Lord Jesus Christ. The reasoning for this conclusion is simple: If Jesus is the Christ, if He is the Only Begotten Son of God and the Savior of the world, then He is the only way to salvation. "I am the way, the truth, and the life," He said, "no man cometh unto the Father, but by me" (John 14:6). If Jesus is the Christ, then His gospel is the only true path to heaven, and only in His true Church can we hope to find salvation. To say otherwise is to suggest there are alternative saviors or other possible routes to heaven besides Jesus Christ and His gospel. To take such a position is to subtly deny Christ and His Atonement. The Savior did not suffer in Gethsemane and die on the cross so that we could say it does not matter what you believe or what path you follow for salvation.

Likewise, we cannot yield on this point because to do so is also to deny the mission and message of the Prophet Joseph Smith. Again, the reasoning is simple: If Joseph Smith truly is the prophet called to restore the Church of Jesus Christ after apostasy, then The Church of Jesus Christ of Latter-day Saints which he restored is the only true path to heaven and our only hope of salvation in the latter days. To say otherwise, to suggest that there are other true churches, is to say that there really was no apostasy and therefore no need for a restoration. To take such a position is to subtly deny the mission of Joseph Smith and the message of the Restoration. "Yield on this doctrine," President Packer warned, "and you cannot justify the Restoration" ("The Only True Church," 82). To do so is to betray the very reason we do missionary work, leaving us without a message worth sharing and our investigators without a church worth joining. The Father and the Son did not appear to the Prophet Joseph Smith so that we could say that all Christian churches are true, and it does not matter which we join.

We cannot yield on this point because to do so leaves us with nothing to offer. As President Packer commented, "Some have recommended that we confine ourselves strictly to evidences of the gospel: happy family life, and temperate living, and so on," while avoiding the message that the true Church has been restored ("The Only True Church," 81). Can we not see what a contradiction this is? As President Gordon B. Hinckley pointed out, "They would pluck the fruit from the tree while cutting off the root from which it grows" ("Joseph Smith Jr.—Prophet of God, Mighty Servant," *Ensign*, December 2005, 2). We must remember that the fruits of our faith grow out of the roots of our religion and that there will never be any meaningful understanding of our fruits without an examination of our roots. Our focus on family, the Word of Wisdom, Church welfare, or any of our inspired programs, all these "evidences" of the gospel grow out of the same foundation. That foundation is the Restoration of the Church of Jesus Christ through the Prophet Joseph Smith. It is *because* this is the only true Church that we have these "evidences" to offer.

Another reason we cannot yield on this point is that, if we do, we lose the Spirit and power of God. As missionaries, we are promised the *Spirit* of the Lord inasmuch as we proclaim the *message* of the Lord. That message is that the gospel of Jesus Christ has been restored through the Prophet Joseph Smith and is found in the one true Church. When we compromise our position as the only true Church, we betray that message and lose the Spirit. But on the other hand, "if we can stand without shame, without hesitancy, without embarrassment, without reservation to bear witness that the gospel has been restored . . . the Lord's Spirit will be with us. And that assurance can be affirmed to others" (Boyd K. Packer, "The Only True Church," 83).

For those who say that we should not proclaim that this is the only true Church because it offends people, we should respond: "To yield on this point would offend God." We know that it is offensive to some; it always has been. It was offensive to the first preacher Joseph Smith shared it with, when he rehearsed the account of the First Vision. This doctrine continued to be a source of persecution throughout his life, ultimately leading to his death. So why did he continue to share it? Because it was true, and he cared more about offending God than offending man. "I had seen a vision; I knew it, and I knew that God knew it, and I could not deny it, neither dared I do it; at least I knew that by so doing I would offend God, and come under condemnation" (JS—H 1:25). We continue to share it today for the same reason. President Packer said, "Popularity and the approval of the world perhaps must remain ever beyond our reach" ("The Only True Church," 82).

For those who consider it uncharitable, unkind, or un-Christlike to proclaim that this is the only true Church, we should respond: "To yield on this point would be uncharitable, unkind, and un-Christlike." Let us not forget that it was Christ Himself who first declared that this is the only true Church (see D&C 1:30), and He is the standard for what is Christlike, loving, and kind. And so we must pause to ask ourselves, *If He is so loving and kind, why would Jesus Christ ever say something so potentially offensive?*

The answer is simple—because He loves us enough to risk offending us for the hope of saving us. When the Lord declared that this is the only true Church, He did that out of kindness and love, not meanness and spite. He wasn't trying to upset people; He was trying to save them. It was not meant as an insult to those of other churches, but as an invitation for them to join His.

When someone is going down the wrong path, the Christlike thing to do is not to cheer them on their way or pretend like they are not lost, but rather to point them in the right direction. If our neighbor's house were on fire, the Christlike thing to do is to warn them, not fear that the news might upset them. We proclaim this doctrine for the same reason, believing that the most Christlike, kind, and loving thing we can do is to offer salvation to erring souls, as it is found only in the one true Church of Jesus Christ.

We cannot yield on this point because to do so is to risk losing potential converts. We teach that we are the only true Church because we believe that "there are many yet on the earth among all [these churches] . . . who are only kept from *the truth* because they know not where to find it" (D&C 123:12; emphasis added). "The truth," as indicated in this verse, is found in its fulness and purity only in this Church. And if we do not openly and plainly declare that the truth of salvation can be found only in the true Church, then they may never know where to find it. How sad it would be to find out that there were many would-be converts who, because we yielded on this doctrine, never joined the true church because, even after talking to the missionaries, "they [knew] not where to find it" (D&C 123:12).

We cannot yield on this point because to do so is to fail in our mission. As missionaries, we are true messengers of the Father. Our mission is to deliver the message we have been entrusted. Just as the mailman has no right to edit, screen, or tamper with the mail—even if he thinks it is bad news, so we have no right to edit, screen, or tamper with the word of the Lord. This is why we must never avoid, dismiss, explain away, or apologize for the Lord's pronouncement that this is His "only true and living church" (D&C 1:30). We, as missionaries, can learn a great lesson from the Lord who, just a few verses after first proclaiming this to be the only true Church, declared, "What I the Lord have spoken, I have spoken, *and I excuse not myself*" (D&C 1:38; emphasis added).

"Boldness, but Not Overbearance"

Though we do not yield on this point and we make no excuses for what the Lord has declared about this Church, we still want to be careful how we share this doctrine. A classic illustration of this comes from President Boyd K. Packer. While serving as mission president in New England, he prepared a beautiful cake for his missionaries. Across the top of the cake was inscribed "The Gospel." When a missionary volunteered to be the first to have a piece, President Packer reached into the cake with his hand, tore out a large piece, and threw it to the elder, splattering some frosting on the elder's suit. In disbelief, none of the other missionaries accepted any more cake when offered it.

Then President Packer carefully cut a slice, placed it with great dignity on a crystal dish with a linen napkin, and asked if anyone else would like a piece. "The lesson was obvious. It was the same cake in both cases, the same flavor, the same nourishment. The manner of serving either made it inviting, even enticing, or uninviting, even revolting. The cake, we reminded the missionaries, represented the gospel. How were they serving it?" (*Teach Ye Diligently* [Salt Lake City: Deseret Book, 1991], 227–28).

The message that this is the only true Church is not something we want to throw in people's faces. We don't use this doctrine as a hammer or a club to hit people over the head with. This is not something we boast or brag about. In teaching it, we never want to come across like the prideful and arrogant Zoramites, whose prayer was, "We thank thee, O God, for we are a chosen people unto thee, while others shall perish" (Alma 31:28). Membership in the Church is not an exclusive status that we hold over peoples' heads; rather, it is a privilege and a blessing that we invite all to receive. After all, this is the kingdom of God, not a country club.

This is why Joseph Smith counseled missionaries to "go in all meekness . . . not to contend with others on account of their faith, or systems of religion, but to pursue a steady course. This I deliver by way of commandment, and all who observe it not will pull down persecution upon their heads, while those who do shall always be filled with the Holy Ghost" (*Teachings of the Prophet Joseph Smith*, 109).

And so the balance—if we are to be the Lord's true messengers, then we must not only say what He would say but we must say it in the same Spirit with which He would say it. This means we must testify that this is His only true Church in the spirit of both courage and kindness, with power and with meekness, using "boldness, but not overbearance" (Alma 38:12), being direct but out of love (see D&C 121:43).

President Gordon B. Hinckley offered some helpful instruction on this matter, and by so doing also provided an example of how to teach this sensitive but essential doctrine. Consider how he blends both power and humility when he shared the following: "The Lord said that this is the only true and living church upon the face of the earth with which He is well pleased [see D&C 1:30]. I didn't say that. Those are His words. The Prophet Joseph was told that the other sects were wrong (see JS—H 1:19). Those are not my words. Those are the Lord's words. But they are hard words for those of other faiths. We don't need to exploit them. We just need to be kind and good and gracious people to others, showing by our example the great truth of that which we believe" (Gordon B. Hinckley, as quoted in "Inspirational Thoughts," *Ensign*, June 2004, 2).

What a beautiful example for us, provided by a prophet of God. It illustrates how to hold our ground while maintaining our tact and how to be sensitive to others as we serve the Lord. President Hinckley did not compromise the message that there is one true Church; instead, he boldly declared it as the word of the Lord. At the same time, though, he did not exploit the doctrine or use it to attack other churches; instead, he called on us to be kind and gracious as we share it with our words and show it by our example. May we follow that powerful example set forth by that beloved prophet.

In the end, we must remember that "we did not invent the doctrine of the only true church. It came from the Lord. Whatever perception others have of us, however presumptuous we appear to be, whatever criticism is directed to us, we must teach it to all who will listen" (Boyd K. Packer, "The Only True Church," 82).

And so we testify to all the world that the one true Church of Jesus Christ has been restored to the earth. And as we do, "there is always the hope, and often it is true, that one among them with an open mind may admit one simple thought: 'Could it possibly be true?' Combine that thought with sincere prayer, and one more soul enters a private sacred grove to find the answer to 'Which of all the churches is true, and which should I join?'" (Boyd K. Packer, "The Only True Church," 83).

6

THE BIBLE:
COMMON GROUND OR
BATTLEGROUND?

I **was interrupted** one afternoon with an urgent request from a fellow seminary teacher: "Brother Mathews, there's a young man from the high school who is interested in the Church and wants to ask the seminary teachers some questions. Since you know the Bible so well, I was wondering if you wanted to join in on the discussion."

I couldn't resist the invitation to do a little missionary work, but the nature of the invitation concerned me. What kind of discussion was this going to be, and why did he think my knowledge of the Bible would be helpful?

It was not long before the answers to these questions were obvious. The boy who came to ask questions was not as sincere as we had been led to believe. In fact, he appeared to have no other intention than to engage the seminary teachers in a good old-fashioned Bible bash. He had clearly done his homework. (Later, he even admitted to being instructed by his priest on what to say.) The other teacher, eager to help answer this young man's "questions," fell quickly into the trap, and they got straight to business. Their conversation went something like this:

Young man: "So, you believe that God has a body. Why do you believe that?"

Seminary Teacher: "Well, the Bible says in Genesis 1:27 that God created man in his own image. Therefore, God must have a body."

Young man: "So you believe that is literal. If you are going to believe everything in the Bible is literal, then you must also believe that God has wings (Ruth 2:12) and that he is a ball of fire (Hebrews 12:29)."

Seminary Teacher: "No, we don't believe that. Those scriptures are speaking figuratively, not literally."

Young man: "Then how do you know that our being created in the image of God is not also figurative and not to be interpreted literally?"

The conversation went on like this for well over an hour. Each time the young man raised a "question," my friend tried to answer it from the Bible, assuming that the Bible was "common ground" and would help them come to an agreement. With each response he gave, the young man disagreed with the interpretation. What my friend called literal, the young man called figurative, and vice versa. No conclusion was ever going to be reached. Both only became more entrenched in his own position. They might still be there if the conversation hadn't been interrupted.

Unfortunately, this story is not uncommon. In fact, it illustrates one of the most common mistakes in missionary work—the assumption that the Bible is common ground among competing Christian churches and can be used to establish truth and prove which church is true. I have even heard well-intentioned Church members counsel young missionaries on their way to the Bible Belt of the southern United States that they need to really know their Bible if they are going to convert anyone. Too often we approach missionary work with this naïve expectation and assume that because we both believe the Bible we can use it to reach consensus and agreement with those not of our faith. We then give exclusive attention to the Bible and avoid teaching from the additional scriptures and revelations of the Restoration, like the First Vision and the Book of Mormon, because our investigators don't already believe those things.

Stop. Before adopting such an approach, we need to understand that this idea is not new; we have not invented it. It has been tried over and over again. It was the chief missionary approach by Christian churches for hundreds of years. By experience, we know it doesn't work. It doesn't work because the Bible, so frequently described as "'common ground,' [is] nothing of the kind—unfortunately it [is] battleground" and has been for centuries (Jeffrey R. Holland, "'My Words . . . Never Cease,'" 92).

Perhaps the best way to show that the Bible is more battleground than common ground is by simply pointing out how many different Christian churches there are. It is estimated that there are close to forty thousand different Christian denominations and churches. Interestingly, all of these churches claim to believe in the Bible, yet none of them agree on what the Bible actually means. Not only do they disagree, but also their disagreements over the interpretation of the Bible are so severe that they feel it necessary to break away and form their own separate churches. Centuries of these arguments over the interpretation of the Bible have led to the creation of thousands and thousands of different Christian churches. Each one of these almost forty thousand churches stands as proof that the Bible is a battleground (not common ground) and is not sufficient in determining which church is true.

Despite this obvious conclusion, Christian missionaries for centuries have used this approach of relying exclusively on the Bible to "prove" their church true. A perfect illustration of this is found in Joseph Smith's account of the events that led up to the First Vision. It provides a great example of how *not* to share the gospel. "My mind at times was greatly excited," explained young Joseph, "the cry and tumult were so great and incessant. The Presbyterians were most decided against the Baptists and Methodists, and used all the powers of both reason and sophistry to prove their errors, or, at least, to make the people think they were in error. On the other hand, the Baptists and Methodists in their turn were equally zealous in endeavoring to establish their own tenets and disprove all others" (JS—H 1:9).

Notice what these missionaries of other churches were doing. Joseph said they were using "reason . . . to prove" their church was true and "disprove all others." Obviously, their tool in this effort was the Bible, and today this method of missionary work is often called "Bible bashing." Not only was this approach ineffective, but also Joseph Smith characterized it as a "war of words and tumult of opinions" and said that it only left him "in darkness and confusion" (JS—H 1:10, 13).

Most of us would probably not want our own missionary efforts described that way, yet how often have we been guilty of this same practice of Bible bashing? How often have we engaged in this war of words that results from trying to prove our beliefs by reasoning from the Bible? If this approach was not effective in converting Joseph Smith, what makes us think that it will be any more effective with our investigators?

It was in part because of these bad experiences with Bible-bashing missionaries that Joseph Smith came to the inspired conclusion for why the Bible isn't effective in establishing which church is true. It is because "the teachers of religion of the different sects understood the same passages of scripture so differently as to destroy all confidence in settling the question [of which church is true] by an appeal to the Bible" (JS—H 1:12). You can't settle this by an appeal to the Bible. That is why no one will ever win a Bible bash. They cannot convincingly prove who is right from a book that everyone understands and interprets "so differently."

As illustrated in the story at the beginning of this chapter, what one person interprets as figurative from the Bible, another may interpret as literal. What someone interprets to mean one thing, another may interpret it to mean something else. And because there are as many interpretations of the Bible as there are readers of the Bible, the Bible alone will never be used to successfully determine which church is true. It was not from the Bible that Joseph Smith discovered the true church, and it will not be from the Bible that our investigators will discover it either.

A More Effective Approach:
Rely on Latter-day Revelation

If the answer to the question of "Which church is true?" is not found in the Bible, where then can it be found? Joseph Smith concluded that the only way to discover which church is true is by gaining "more wisdom" (JS—H 1:12), by receiving more revelation. As explained earlier in this book, what this means for missionaries is that the way we answer the question of "Which church is true?" is not by appealing to what they already have in the Bible, but rather by introducing them to more, through latter-day revelation. This means relying on the First Vision, the Book of Mormon, and other scriptures and revelations of the Restoration to present our message. It was through these latter-day revelations that Joseph Smith discovered the true Church, and it will be through latter-day revelations that our investigators discover it also.

If the preachers of religion in Joseph's day are good illustrations of what *not* to do, then the Father and the Son are the perfect examples of what we *should* do in effective missionary work. They were the first missionaries in this dispensation, and Joseph Smith was their first convert. When They taught him, They did not rely on reasoning from the Bible in establishing Their doctrine, even though all They taught perfectly conforms with it. Instead, They simply taught Joseph through latter-day revelation by presenting the First Vision, and later the Book of Mormon and additional latter-day revelations. What better example could we have than from God?

Our job as missionaries is to follow that example. We are to rely on latter-day revelation in teaching our message. This approach is based on the simple notion that the best way to teach our message that God speaks in our day is by *showing people what He has actually said in our day*, not by inferring it from Bible verses (that show God used to speak a long time ago).

We believe the Bible. We state that as an article of faith. That is not the issue. At issue is whether the Bible is the primary tool God intended that we use to present His message in missionary work.

As Elder Bruce R. McConkie has explained,

> It has been our traditional course in days past, unfortunately all too frequently, to say, "Here is the Bible, and the Bible says this and this, and therefore the gospel has been restored.". . . [But] it is not the Bible that brings people into the Church; it is the Book of Mormon and latter-day revelation . . . until we get involved with latter-day revelation, the process of conversion does not begin to operate in any substantial degree in the heart of an investigator. . . .
>
> Our message is one of latter-day revelation, and we use latter-day revelation to present it to the world. We use the Bible as a supplement. . . .
>
> It is not what came to Peter, James, and John that will save us, even though they had exactly what has now been given to us. Salvation comes through living prophets. You can't be baptized by a dead prophet. You have to find the living oracles who are the legal administrators for our day. This is why people's attention has to be centered in latter-day revelation. ("Seven Steps to More and Better Converts," Mission Presidents' Seminar, June 21, 1975)

What this means is that instead of following the traditional course of presenting our message primarily from the Bible, we should rely on latter-day revelation. For example, instead of trying to prove that God has a body by going to Genesis and reading a verse that says we are created in His image, it would be more effective to simply teach the First Vision, where God reveals His image in plainness. Instead of going to the writings of Paul in an attempt to prove there was an apostasy, why not go to the First Vision, where the Lord stated clearly that there had been an apostasy? Instead of reading 1 and 2 Corinthians as evidence of degrees of glory, why not teach Doctrine and Covenants 76 and let our investigators feel the Spirit of that tremendous vision of Christ and the degrees of glory? Instead of going to Ezekiel or John or Revelation to prove the Book of Mormon is true, wouldn't it be more effective to just invite people to read it and find out for themselves?

After all, that's how Joseph Smith learned these things. Joseph Smith didn't come to the conclusion that God looked like a man in form by reading it in Genesis; he didn't discover that there had been an apostasy by reading Paul's epistles; he didn't come to believe in degrees of glory or baptisms for the dead or the Book of Mormon or any of our unique doctrines by discovering them in some obscure passage from the Bible (and neither will our investigators!). Joseph Smith learned all of these things from latter-day revelation. Then, *after* they had been revealed to him, he discovered that they were supported in the Bible.

As missionaries, we should teach our investigators the same way that the Lord taught Joseph Smith. We should train ourselves to teach God's message first from latter-day revelation, and *then*, when necessary, share the appropriate Bible verse to *support* what we have taught (see D&C 35:23). As *Preach My Gospel* counsels, "Give priority to Book of Mormon passages when you teach, but also show how the Book of Mormon and the Bible teach the same principles" (*Preach My Gospel*, 106).

Perhaps the best way to visualize why we should take this approach in missionary work and give priority to Book of Mormon passages and other latter-day revelations is demonstrated by a simple illustration provided by Elder Tad R. Callister. The illustration goes like this,

> How many straight lines can you draw through a single point on a piece of paper? The answer is infinite. For a moment, suppose that single point represents the Bible and that hundreds of those straight lines drawn through that point represent different interpretations of the Bible and that each of those interpretations represents a different church.

What happens, however, if on that piece of paper there is a second point representing the Book of Mormon? How many straight lines could you draw between these two reference points: the Bible and the Book of Mormon? Only one. Only one interpretation of Christ's doctrines survives the testimony of these two witnesses.

Again and again the Book of Mormon acts as a confirming, clarifying, unifying witness of the doctrines taught in the Bible so that there is only "one Lord, one faith, one baptism." ("The Book of Mormon—A Book from God," *Ensign*, November 2011, 75)

As this illustration shows, without latter-day revelation, the interpretation of the Bible remains ambiguous, subject to endless interpretation, and never fully able to answer the question of which church is true. But when latter-day revelation, namely the Book of Mormon, is introduced into the discussion, the interpretation of the Bible becomes plain and clear, and we can agree on its meaning. Only when we rely on latter-day revelation does the choice of which church to join become obvious to the honest in heart. This is why it is easier to convert a person with the Book of Mormon than it is to convince them of what the Bible really means.

Some might object to this approach of emphasizing latter-day revelation over the Bible in missionary work by saying, "But they don't believe in the Book of Mormon and other latter-day revelations. How can we use *that* in a discussion?" No, they don't believe in it, and they never will if we don't introduce them to it. And isn't that the whole purpose of our missionary efforts anyway? Where does it say that we are limited to only talking about what they already believe? Isn't our purpose to teach them something new? Furthermore, if they really are unwilling to even consider the possibility of latter-day revelation, then they can never begin the "experiment upon [the] word" that is required for them to find out for themselves (Alma 32:27). People who are that hardened to the truth will never know which church is true, and no amount of Bible bashing will change that.

Establishing Peace by Using Latter-day Revelation

Sadly, so many well-intentioned missionaries have relied exclusively on the Bible and downplay latter-day revelation because they think it will bring peace, when in reality it so often brings war (JS—H 1:9–10). As we have seen, the Bible is not common ground, "unfortunately, it [is] battleground" (Holland, *Ensign*, May 2008, 92). Ironically, the peace they seek is found in the very thing they are afraid to share: latter-day revelation. The Book of Mormon was prophesied to come forth "unto the confounding of false doctrines and laying down of contentions, and *establishing peace*" (2 Nephi 3:12; emphasis added). By clarifying the Bible, the Book of Mormon brings peace by ending the Bible bash. No longer is there any reason to argue and debate over how to interpret the Bible because latter-day revelation provides the interpretation. Our investigators can believe our testimony or not, but there is nothing to argue about. When we rely on latter-day revelation, we leave the fight.

A story that illustrates this point is shared by one former mission president who had challenged his missionaries at zone conference to rely on latter-day revelation and teach from the Book of Mormon and the Doctrine and Covenants. He explained,

> I told them that any principle that they could not teach from those sources they had no business teaching because it was not a part of the message that the Lord had commissioned us to take to the ends of the earth. It seemed a reasonable assumption to us that if the gospel had indeed been restored and we in reality represented a new gospel dispensation, then we could teach the message as the Lord had given it to us.
>
> Between then and our next round of zone conferences, the reports flooded in. The missionaries spoke of a stronger spirit in their meetings, even to the point of being overwhelming. It was obvious that the Holy Ghost liked being a part of what they were doing. Their confidence increased when they knew they were standing on their own ground. Naturally, they found more people to teach than they ever had before. These things I expected, but I did not expect the report that the spirit of contention, common to many efforts to teach, was now gone. After our one-month experiment, our missionaries refused to return to their old methods. Their faith was centered in the revelations of the Restoration. They liked the spirit of the whole thing.
>
> The missionaries conceded that they did not necessarily know any more about the Bible than did those they taught. There was no reason to argue over the meaning of Bible passages, which was not their message. Their message was that God had spoken through a living prophet, and they stuck to that message. When those they were

teaching understood this, they asked questions about what God had told the Prophet about this or that, and with every question came the opportunity to open the revelations of the Restoration and let their light shine. That light carries its own spirit. One can accept it or reject it, but one cannot argue with it. (Joseph Fielding McConkie, "The First Vision and Religious Tolerance" in *A Witness for the Restoration*, ed. Kent P. Jackson and Andrew C. Skinner [Provo, Utah: Religious Studies Center, Brigham Young University, 2007], 177–99)

As this story shows, relying on latter-day revelation can actually help us avoid contention and establish peace. In fact, latter-day revelation, beginning with the First Vision, is really the God-given resolution to the Bible bash. Think about it for a moment. As long as God doesn't speak to clarify His word, then how to interpret the Bible is all a matter of opinion, and everyone's opinion is equally valid. But if God speaks today through latter-day revelation proves, then the debate over how to interpret His word is over. Therefore, the Bible bash should have ended in the Sacred Grove, when God spoke again through latter-day revelation. No longer is there an infinite number of ways to interpret the Bible; there is only one way—His way. No longer is there any need to speculate or argue about what God meant in the Bible because He has explained it clearly through latter-day revelation and living prophets. We do not have to put words in His mouth; He can speak for Himself. And because God speaks today, the debate is over if we will but "hear Him!" (JS—H 1:17).

When we understand this, we come to a very important conclusion. Bible bashing is wrong not only because it is contentious, but also because it denies latter-day revelation and misses the whole point of the Restoration! If all the answers were clearly stated in the Bible, as we assume when we Bible bash, then why the need for more revelation? Why the need for the Book of Mormon, or for the Restoration? When we Bible bash, we contradict our whole message by reverting back to 1820, pretending like God never has spoken by latter-day revelation, and dismissing the whole Restoration.

Do we not see that this is a trap? By limiting us to the Bible, Satan has already won? When we accept his challenge to prove all of our beliefs from the Bible and dismiss or ignore latter-day revelation, it is as if there never were a Restoration. This is exactly what Satan wants. It is his subtle way of perpetuating the Apostasy and maintaining the power he once had over all mankind while they were in a state of ignorance and confusion, arguing over the Bible. This power he lost in the Sacred Grove (but not without a fight! see JS—H 1:16), and we freely give this power right back to him when we dismiss latter-day revelation and choose to Bible bash. When will we see that latter-day revelation is the only way out of this fight, and that by avoiding latter-day revelation, we are doomed to argue forever about the Bible in a state of confusion and apostasy?

I was grateful that I had learned these lessons from modern prophets when I found myself in the missionary discussion mentioned at the start of this chapter. As a result, I could help end the Bible bash and center their attention on latter-day revelation. And so, after going round and round in a fruitless and seemingly endless debate over how to interpret the Bible, finally I jumped in and said, "Did it ever occur to either of you that the question of which church is true cannot be answered from the Bible? And that this whole discussion confirms that?"

Stunned, they both turned to me. Now that I had their attention, I opened up to Joseph Smith—History and compared what they were doing to the "war of words" Joseph Smith described in his day and explained that this argument has been going on for centuries and is the reason why there are so many Christian churches.

Then I explained from verse 12 that because of the differences of opinion about how to interpret the Bible, Joseph Smith concluded that the question of which church was true could not be answered from the Bible, and so this debate we were having was useless. Then, with all the energy of my soul, I taught the First Vision and explained that if he wanted to know which church was true, he would have to do as Joseph Smith did and ask of God. I invited him to do so and suggested that one way he could investigate whether Joseph Smith really saw God would be by studying the Book of Mormon. I closed with my testimony.

The First Vision is latter-day revelation. The Book of Mormon is latter-day revelation. Individual testimony comes by personal, latter-day revelation. Revelation, revelation, revelation. That is our message to all the world, and we should use latter-day revelation to teach it. The Bible is not the common ground we assume it is—it is battleground. The truth is that we do not really seek to share common ground with the world. We stand independent (see D&C 78:14 and Boyd K. Packer, "The Only True Church," 82). We stand on the ground of latter-day revelation. We stand with living prophets. We stand in the Sacred Grove and on the Hill Cumorah. As missionaries, we invite all the world to stand with us.

The next day, my friend and fellow seminary teacher approached me and thanked me for what I had shared. He then turned to me thoughtfully and said, "I will never do missionary work the same way again."

That was my reaction when I first learned this powerful principle, and I hope it will be the reaction of every member and missionary who ever discovers it. The more this simple principle takes root in our hearts, the more powerful and effective we will be at sharing the gospel, because it will inspire us to leave the battleground of the Bible bash and rely more on latter-day revelation.

7

THE BIBLE: A
SEALED BOOK

Just before I left on my mission to Guatemala, a well-intentioned friend gave me a gift. The gift was a popular little reference book for missionaries. It was organized by topic and filled with Bible "proof texts," verses intended to prove our various beliefs from the Bible. I remember that I had every intention of packing this book and am even quite sure that I did. But when my trainer asked if I had a copy he could use, I searched my bags, and it was nowhere to be found. I count that as one of the best mistakes I have ever made. (I sometimes wonder if it was removed by angels!) Had it not been for that inspired error, I might have beem led to to Bible-bash instead of becoming a missionary of the restored gospel.

It is easy to see how someone could naively believe that relying on Bible verses to prove our point would be effective in missionary work. The reasoning is simple enough: Our Christian friends believe the Bible, and so do we. If we show them a verse that supports our beliefs, surely they will agree, right? But as we have just seen in the previous chapter, it is one thing to believe the same Bible; it is another to interpret it the same way. But why do people interpret the Bible "so differently" (JS—H 1:12)? Why is it that they do not see what we see in the pages of the book? The reason that people interpret the Bible so differently is because "the Bible as we now have it is a sealed book" (Bruce R. McConkie, "The Bible, a Sealed Book," address given at CES Symposium, August 17, 1984). It is not sealed in the same sense as the portion of the Book of Mormon was sealed; it is not that man can't read it, but rather it is closed or locked to man's understanding. Because the Bible is a sealed book to the world, it is often a source of confusion and contention. What happened to the Bible to cause this seal of confusion is one of the great mysteries revealed in the Book of Mormon.

How the Bible Became a Sealed Book

Nephi, in his great vision of the future, saw that after the death of Christ, "the world" would be "gathered together to fight against the twelve apostles" (1 Nephi 11:35), eventually resulting in the loss of the New Testament Christian church. He then saw that the Church established among his own people (the Nephites) would have a similar fate (see 1 Nephi 12:15–23). Then, after the true Church of Jesus Christ was no longer on the earth, Nephi "saw among the nations of the Gentiles the formation of a great church . . . which is most abominable above all other churches" (1 Nephi 13:4–5). What is typically meant by the great and abominable church or church of the devil is "every evil and worldly organization on earth that perverts the pure and perfect gospel and fights against the Lamb of God [Jesus Christ]" (Guide to the Scriptures, "Devil, church of"). A classic example of this usage of the term is found in the very next chapter, where Nephi is told that "there are save two churches only; the one is the church of the Lamb of God, and the other is the church of the devil" (1 Nephi 14:10). Obviously, this term is being used here with a very broad meaning and includes all the forces in the world that oppose the true Church of Jesus Christ and its teachings.

However, on other occasions in the scriptures, the term "church of the devil" can focus more narrowly on a specific manifestation of Satan's influence and power through a particular organization or event in history. This is the case in 1 Nephi 13. Here, the scriptures are clearly referring to something a little more specific than "every evil and worldly organization," because they state that this "church" is more abominable than all other false churches. It doesn't make sense to say "all false churches" are more abominable than "all other false churches." Obviously, these verses are singling something out. Some specific entity existed in that day that was more abominable and destructive than all the other forces of evil. From Nephi's description, we can discover what this is referring to by identifying the specific time and place in which this particular force of evil wielded its power.

The timing of these prophesied events must be prior to the discovery of America (see 1 Nephi 13:12) but after the true Church of Jesus Christ had been lost from the earth (see 1 Nephi 11–12) in the period of time that we sometimes call the Dark Ages. It is clear that this "church" wielded great power and was responsible for religious oppression and even murder during that time period (see 1 Nephi 13:5–9). The location where this "church" wielded its power to oppress and destroy was primarily among the "mother" nations of Europe, whose pilgrims sought refuge from their religious captivity by fleeing to the promised land of America (see 1 Nephi 13:13–17). What organization or event wielded such great power to oppress and destroy throughout the Dark Ages in Europe? For those who know history, the answer is clear. A footnote to this term found later in the chapter helps us solve the mystery and identify the specific manifestation of the church of the devil being prophesied of here. The footnote refers the reader to the topic of "apostasy of the early Christian church" (see footnote to 1 Nephi 13:26d).

It was specifically apostate Christianity that Nephi was describing in 1 Nephi 13. "The historical abominable church of the devil [referred to in 1 Nephi 13] is that apostate church that replaced true Christianity in the first and second centuries, teaching the philosophies of men mingled with scriptures. It dethroned God in the church and replaced him with man by denying the principle of revelation and turning instead to human intellect" (Stephen E. Robinson, "Warring against the Saints of God," Ensign, January 1988, 39). Apostate Christianity in that time period was not limited to a single denomination; rather, it embraced all the corrupt groups, organizations, and secret combinations that usurped power after the apostles died and used their religious influence to oppress and destroy. They were the ones historically responsible for the many atrocities witnessed in Nephi's vision. It must have been sad for Nephi to learn that it was the corrupted form of the very Church Christ established that would bring upon the world such spiritual bondage.

The religious oppression produced by apostate Christianity was a "yoke of iron" (1 Nephi 13:5) that prevailed in Europe and was largely responsible for the Dark Ages. Part of this religious oppression was caused by withholding access to the Bible from the common people. As Elder M. Russell Ballard has explained, "The Dark Ages were dark because the light of the gospel was hidden from the people. They did not have the apostles or prophets, nor did they have access to the Bible. The clergy kept the scriptures secret and unavailable to the people" ("The Miracle of the Holy Bible," *Ensign*, May 2007, 80). What Nephi saw really happened in history, and we must understand what he was describing if we are going to appreciate what he saw next in his vision. We cannot appreciate the religious freedom offered in America if we do not understand the religious oppression that existed in Europe. Likewise, we cannot appreciate the Restoration if we do not fully understand the Great Apostasy and its effects upon mankind.

It was in their attempt to escape the religious bondage and spiritual oppression of apostate Christianity that the people of Europe fled to the religious freedom promised in America (see 1 Nephi 13:13). When these pilgrims came to America, Nephi noticed that they arrived with "a book" which was "carried forth among them" (1 Nephi 13:20). The book he saw was the Holy Bible, and it was a miracle that they had the Bible with them. As Elder M. Russell Ballard declared,

> The Holy Bible is a miracle! . . . [It is a miracle that it] was protected through the Dark Ages and through the conflicts of countless generations so that we may have it today. . . . It is not by chance or coincidence that we have the Bible today. Righteous individuals were prompted by the Spirit to record both the sacred things they saw and the inspired words they heard and spoke. Other devoted people were prompted to protect and preserve these records. Men like John Wycliffe, the courageous William Tyndale, and Johannes Gutenberg were prompted against much opposition to translate the Bible into language people could understand and to publish it in books people could read. . . . We owe much to the many brave martyrs and reformers like Martin Luther, John Calvin, and John Huss who demanded freedom to worship and common access to the holy books. . . . We must ever remember the countless martyrs who knew of its power and who gave their lives that we may be able to [have it]. ("The Miracle of the Holy Bible," 80)

We have the Bible today because faithful men and women wrestled it free from the dominant churches of apostate Christianity. The Bible they produced was basically a pirated copy that was translated into the common languages and smuggled into the hands of the people. Many faithful people died so that we could have the Bible. But what Nephi sees in his vision shows that it was all worth it, because it implies that it was the influence of the Bible that inspired these pilgrims to leave their homelands, cross an ocean, and settle a continent. It was the Bible that inspired them to seek for a promised land where they could freely worship God like they read about in the Bible. It was the Bible that inspired the formation of this great nation. And it would be the Bible that would inspire a young Joseph Smith to "ask of God" and begin the Restoration (JS—H 1:11–13). It is hard to overstate the importance of the Bible and its influence upon mankind.

Despite the great worth of the Holy Bible and the miracle that it was preserved for us, it is here in Nephi's vision that we learn that it was not preserved for us in its purity. The Bible, Nephi was told, was originally written "in purity . . . according to the truth which is in God" (1 Nephi 13:25). The angel explained that "when it proceeded forth from the mouth of a Jew it *contained* the fulness of the gospel" (1 Nephi 13:24; emphasis added).

But something happened to it. Something corrupted it. Something happened that forced the angel to say it *contained* rather than *contains* the fulness of the gospel. After it left the hands of its original prophetic authors, it fell into the hands of "the great and abominable church," and "they have taken away from the gospel of the Lamb many parts which are plain and most precious" (1 Nephi 13:26, 28). This is what has made it a sealed book to the world.

It is important to recognize that these fundamental and saving gospel truths were not only accidentally lost in translation, but often deliberately and intentionally "taken away" long before there was any attempt at translation (1 Nephi 13:26). Regardless of how good a translator is, if the text they receive is incomplete, then there will be problems with the translation. These truths that were taken from the Bible were selected because of their content. They were removed because they plainly exposed Satan's lies and contradicted the things he wanted taught by apostate Christianity. It is as if Satan had the opportunity in some cases to edit the Bible and take out some things he didn't like. (Imagine what truths the world would like to take from the Bible today, if they had the chance). Joseph Smith was aware of this problem and explained that "many important points touching the salvation of men, had been taken from the Bible, or lost before it was compiled" (*Teachings of the Prophet Joseph Smith*, 10; quoted also in D&C 76 Introduction). This is what led him later to say, "I believe the Bible as it read when it came from the pen of the original writers," but "ignorant translators, careless transcribers, or designing and corrupt priests have committed many errors" but "ignorant translators, careless transcribers, or designing and corrupt priests have committed many errors" (*Teachings of the Prophet Joseph Smith*, 327; see also Bible Dictionary, "Bible," 624). As a result of this tampering, we as Latter-day Saints feel compelled to say that "we believe the Bible to be the word of God as far *as it is translated correctly*" (Articles of Faith 1:8; emphasis added).

Those deliberately responsible for this fiendish effort are identified in the scriptures simply as "the great and abominable church" (1 Nephi 13:28). Again, it is clear that this is not speaking of all false churches or worldly organizations because most of these today did not even exist at that time and could have had nothing to do with this destructive endeavor. This was done early and, as the footnote indicates, was part of the "apostasy of the early Christian church." Apostate Christianity was responsible for suppressing the word of God, just as they were responsible for oppressing the children of God. That same false spirit that initiated the Apostasy, by inspiring men to betray and murder the Apostles and prophets, that same false spirit tried to finish the job by inspiring others to betray the Apostles' memory and murder their legacy by editing their words and defiling their doctrine. The same spirit that sought to silence them in life sought also to silence them in death.

The intended result of this scripture tampering is a recorded by Nephi in these words: "And all this have they done that they might pervert the right ways of the Lord, that they might blind the eyes and harden the hearts of the children of men" (1 Nephi 13:27). Satan's plot was to remove plainness and clarity from the Bible so that it would be misinterpreted and "mingled with the philosophies of men," allowing him to deceive and control mankind.

Sadly, this conspiracy that was inspired by the devil and accomplished by his followers, was successful. "Because of the many plain and precious things which have been taken out of the [Bible]. . . an exceedingly great many do stumble, yea, insomuch that Satan hath great power over them" (1 Nephi 13:29). Thus, to Satan's benefit, the Bible became a sealed book, sealed by confusion and misunderstanding, sealed because truths that could have clarified its meaning were removed, and sealed because apostles and prophets who could have explained its words were killed.

When we understand what happened to the Bible, we begin to see why so much confusion and ignorance enshroud it and why it is not the most effective resource in missionary work. We expect our investigators to see in its pages the same things we do, when in fact they do not. So much of it is locked to the understanding of the world, as if they are reading it in the dark.

How to Unlock the Sealed Book

How do we solve this problem? What must we do to help our investigators see what we see and understand the Bible the way we do? How do we remove the seals of confusion and misunderstanding from the Bible so that its true meaning is plainly understood? Or will its readers "forever remain in that awful state of blindness" (1 Nephi 13:32)?

The solution is simple. If they are reading in the dark, then we turn on the lights. If the Bible is a sealed book, then we offer them the key to unlock it. The Lord explained to Nephi how this was to be done: "I will be merciful," he said. "I will bring forth" a book that contains "my gospel . . . my rock and my salvation" (1 Nephi 13:33–36). We know this book today as the Book of Mormon: Another Testament of Jesus Christ.

The Book of Mormon contains the "fulness of the gospel of Jesus Christ" (D&C 20:9), meaning that the Book of Mormon contains all the basics of the gospel and provides a foundation for gospel understanding. But the Book of Mormon would not be the only book of scripture sent to restore plain and precious truths. Nephi learned that "other books" of scripture would follow, including the Doctrine and Covenants, Pearl of Great Price, and the Joseph Smith Translation of the Bible, not to mention the printed words of our living prophets found in Church magazines and other publications (see 1 Nephi 13:39). These books would join together to reveal the gospel of Jesus Christ in plainness and purity. By shining the light of this additional revelation upon the Bible, it can be read and understood with unmistakable clarity. If the Bible is a sealed book, then the key to unlock it is latter-day revelation and the scriptures of the Restoration.

Latter-day revelation unlocks the Bible by serving two important functions. First, it confirms that what is in the Bible is true, even if it is incomplete. Nephi was taught that latter-day revelation would be given "unto the convincing of the Gentiles . . . and also the Jews . . . that the records of the prophets and of the twelve apostles of the Lamb [contained in the Bible] are true" (1 Nephi 13:39). It is interesting to notice that while many missionaries spend time ineffectively trying to prove the Book of Mormon true from the Bible, the Lord intended that we do just the opposite. The Book of Mormon was sent to prove that what's in the Bible is true.

The second function of latter-day revelation is to "make known the plain and precious things which have been taken away from [the Bible]" (1 Nephi 13:40). Just as there was a restoration of priesthood by angelic messengers, so there has been a restoration of truth through latter-day scripture. Through these two functions, confirming the truths already in the Bible and restoring additional truths that were lost, latter-day revelation explains and expounds the word of God and unlocks the true meaning of the Bible.

The story of what happened to the Bible and the purpose of latter-day revelation might be illustrated by a simple analogy. It is as if we were given a beautiful, framed portrait of Jesus Christ. If someone wanted to prevent us from enjoying this painting and understanding what it depicts, they wouldn't have to steal it or destroy it. All they would have to do is strategically mar or conceal some of the most important parts so that the painting is left incomplete, and its meaning becomes unclear. Though it still contains *some* of Christ's face, with such a painting you might not be able to recognize the Lord even if you saw Him. This is exactly what Satan did to the Bible through the Apostasy. He did it to confuse the world and make it more challenging for them to recognize the true Christ and His true gospel.

Instead of simply offering us the missing parts to reinsert into the painting, the Lord solves this problem in a more elegant manner. It is as if He provided us with an entirely new portrait; it may have come in a different frame, but it contains the same beautiful painting of Jesus Christ. This second portrait provides perspective to the first and helps us make sense of and interpret what is left of it. In addition, this second painting supplies the vision of what was missing from the first. The true meaning of the original portrait would be understood and the subject of the painting would be recognized. This is exactly what the Book of Mormon and other latter-day revelations do for the Bible.

"In the real and true sense of the word, the only way to understand the Bible is first to gain a knowledge of God's dealings with men through latter-day revelation" (Bruce R. McConkie, "The Bible, a Sealed Book," a Symposium on the New Testament, August 17, 1984). Because of this, when we as Latter-day Saints read the Bible, it as if we are reading a different book, or at least reading it through different eyes. We read it through the lenses of living prophets and latter-day revelation, which gives us an entirely different perspective. We see in it things the rest of the world can't see. For us, the Bible is an open book because the seals have been removed.

When we realize this, we begin to understand why Bible bashing is so pointless and why we shouldn't attempt to prove our beliefs by reasoning from the Bible. We expect others to see the same thing we do, and then we're surprised when they don't. But they are reading in the dark. They are reading a sealed book. If we want people to see what we do, then we need to turn on the lights; we need to give them the key! We do this by introducing them to latter-day revelation. Only then will they see what we see. Only then will they be reading the same book we are.

Joseph Smith, as the ideal investigator, is the perfect pattern of how latter-day revelation unlocks the Bible. His story began with him confused about, among other things, how to interpret the Bible (see JS—H 1:12). He realized quickly that because of the infinite interpretations, the only sure way to interpret it correctly is to "ask of God" for "more wisdom" through direct revelation (JS—H 1:12–13). This he did, and he received the First Vision. Immediately he was introduced to the Father and the Son, the principal Authors of the Bible, and began to better understand such fundamental points as prayer, faith, and revelation. This began to unlock the book to his understanding. Later, he received the Book of Mormon, which contains the fulness of the gospel. This also helped, but what ultimately opened up the Bible to his understanding was given to him just after he was baptized.

"We were filled with the Holy Ghost," he explained. "Our minds being now enlightened, we began to have the scriptures [the Bible] laid open to our understandings, and the true meaning and intention of their more mysterious passages revealed unto us in a manner which we never could attain to previously, nor ever before had thought of"

(JS—H 1:73–74). Joseph Smith didn't feel like he really understood the Bible until after he had been baptized and received the Holy Ghost.

Reflecting on this principle, at the end of his life, Joseph Smith explained, "I thank God that I have got this old book [the Bible]; but I thank him more for the gift of the Holy Ghost. I have got the oldest book in the world; but I [also] have got the oldest book in my heart, even the gift of the Holy Ghost" (*Teachings of the Prophet Joseph Smith*, 349). It was only through the gift of the Holy Ghost and latter-day revelation that Joseph Smith was able to understand the true meaning of the Bible.

As with Joseph, so it will be with us and our investigators. The key to understanding the Bible is latter-day revelation, which is precisely why missionary work should center on latter-day revelation. Only when investigators come to know the prophets and revelations of our day can they really understand the prophets and revelations of days past.

And so they should begin where Joseph Smith began, with the First Vision. This is followed up with exactly what he received next: the Book of Mormon. We invite them to read and pray about it so they can receive their own personal latter-day revelation confirming that these things are true. With this testimony, they join the Church and receive the gift of the Holy Ghost, which is their right to constantly enjoy the spirit of revelation.

With all this latter-day revelation, the Bible will become an open book to them as it is for us. Then, and only then, will they see what we see and recognize how frequently and powerfully the Bible bears witness of the Restoration.

8

JESUS CHRIST AND JOSEPH SMITH

A neighbor of mine once shared an experience that is all too common among those who share the gospel. He is a music teacher, and one of his students was in his home learning the piano. At a break in the instruction, this young woman picked up his hymnbook from on top of the piano and began flipping through the pages. She stopped at the hymn "Praise to the Man" and sneered. Curious at her reaction, my friend asked her why she did that. Her response: "You Mormons worship Joseph Smith." My friend was surprised by her attitude. She must have just seen dozens of hymns of worship for Heavenly Father and Jesus Christ but had decided to focus on this one praising Joseph Smith. Not only that, but she seemed to overlook the true message of the hymn, which is that we sing praise to the man Joseph Smith because he "communed with Jehovah" and because "Jesus anointed that prophet and seer" ("Praise to the Man," *Hymns*, no. 27). She had misunderstood the message. And in this case, it seemed like she did so intentionally.

Many of us will have experiences with those who accuse us of worshipping the Prophet Joseph Smith because we mention him so frequently when we teach the message of the Restoration. Even members of the Church can sometimes become confused about why we talk so much about Joseph Smith, and question whether we should not just teach about the Savior Jesus Christ and not mention the Prophet Joseph Smith so much. As missionaries, we must clearly understand why we teach about Joseph Smith so that we can effectively communicate that reason to others. If it is not clear to us, we can not expect it to be clear to others why the message of Jesus Christ and Joseph Smith must always go hand-in-hand in our missionary efforts.

Christ Revealed through Prophets

Part of the reason some are confused about why we talk so much about Joseph Smith is because the Christian world in general has lost the understanding of the role of prophets. It has simply been so long since they have accepted a true prophet that many have forgotten the purpose for why God sends prophets in the first place. They have assumed that the Bible fills the role of prophets, and therefore most think they don't need any more prophets.

Because the knowledge of the role of prophets was lost during the Apostasy, it was one of the first things the Lord restored in our day. On the day the Church was organized, as the Saints were gathered in their initial sacrament meeting to sustain Joseph Smith as the leader of the Church, the Lord gave a revelation. He wanted to make it clear that Joseph Smith was to be more than just the leader of the Church—he was to be "a prophet" (D&C 21:1). In Hebrew, the word *prophet* means "spokesman," and it denotes that a prophet is to act as a messenger of the Lord (see Bible Dictionary, "Prophet"). The Lord explained this very principle when he gave his first commandment to the newly organized Church. That commandment was basically to follow the prophet. The Lord commanded, "Wherefore, meaning the church, thou shalt give heed unto all his words . . . for his word ye shall receive, as if from mine own mouth" (D&C 21:4–5). As shown here, the Lord commands us to listen to and follow His prophets because their words are His words, as they serve as His spokesmen and messengers. True Saints in the true Church have been striving to obey that command ever since.

Once the role of prophets is clear, it becomes obvious why we talk so much about them. They are the revealers of Christ and His word. We love prophets *because* we love Jesus Christ. And when we talk about prophets, we are talking about Jesus Christ, because their words are His words. As the Lord Himself declared, "Whether by mine own voice or by the voice of my servants, it is the same" (D&C 1:38). Their job is not to replace the Lord, but rather to reveal Him to mankind. Without prophets, we would not have the words of the Lord Jesus Christ. Even those who don't accept modern prophets should be able to understand this concept, for what would they know about Jesus Christ if not for the words of the prophets and apostles in the Bible?

As a result, Christ and His prophets are united as one. As Elder Bruce R. McConkie explained,

> Christ and his prophets go together. They cannot be separated. It is utterly and completely impossible to believe in Christ without also believing in and accepting the divine commission of the prophets sent to reveal him and to carry his saving truths to the world.
>
> No one today would say: "I will believe in Christ, but will not believe in Peter, James, and John and their testimony of him." In the very nature of things belief in Christ is more than accepting him as a single person standing alone, as one person independent of any other. Belief in Christ presupposes and includes within it the acceptance of the prophets who reveal him to the world. (Bruce R. McConkie, in Conference Report, October 1964, 37)

As a result, we cannot talk about Christ without also talking about the prophets He has sent to declare His word and teach His gospel.

Dispensations of the Gospel

When we teach the restored gospel, we not only teach of modern prophets in general, but also specifically speak of Joseph Smith in particular. To understand why Joseph Smith stands out among all the prophets of the latter days requires an examination of the concept of gospel dispensations. In the Bible Dictionary, we learn that "a dispensation of the gospel is a period of time" (Bible Dictionary, "Dispensations"). What distinguishes these discrete periods of earth's history is that they are initiated and headed by a special prophet, an "authorized servant on the earth who bears the holy priesthood and the keys, and who has a divine commission to *dispense the gospel* to the inhabitants of the earth" (Bible Dictionary, "Dispensations"; emphasis added).

If you have ever been to a fast food restaurant, then you already understand the concept of dispensing. There, you will find all kinds of dispensers, from napkin dispensers to ketchup dispensers to straw dispensers. These devices serve to *dispense* or distribute, deliver, and give out their various items. Similarly, the Lord has called special prophets to serve as gospel dispensers, chosen to *dispense* the gospel, or in other words, reveal it anew in their day "so that people of that dispensation do not have to depend basically on past dispensations for knowledge of the plan of salvation" (Bible Dictionary, "Dispensations"). The reason the gospel has been periodically dispensed through a series of restorations is because the gospel has been periodically lost, at least to some degree, through a series of apostasies (see Russell M. Nelson, "The Gathering of Scattered Israel," *Ensign*, November 2006, 79).

Though all the prophets are witnesses of Christ and have authority to teach His gospel, these special prophets, called dispensation heads, are the prophets who first reveal this knowledge and authority again after a period of apostasy. And it is through these dispensation heads that all others in that day must receive the truths of the gospel and authority of the priesthood. As Elder Bruce R. McConkie explained, "Every dispensation head is a revealer of Christ for his day . . . and every other prophet or apostle who comes is a reflection and an echo and an exponent of the dispensation head. All such come to echo to the world and to expound and unfold what God has revealed through the man who was appointed for that era to give his eternal word to the world. Such is the dispensation concept" ("This Generation Shall Have My Word through You," *Ensign*, June 1980, 55). These special prophet-leaders, or dispensation heads, include Adam, Enoch, Noah, Abraham, Moses, Jesus Christ, and Joseph Smith (see Bible Dictionary, "Dispensations"; see also *Preach My Gospel*, 37).

As a result, to accept the gospel in each dispensation requires people to not only gain a testimony of Jesus Christ as the Savior, but also a testimony of the prophet sent to dispense or reveal Christ's gospel in that day. For example, anyone that lived in the days of Adam had to not only accept Jesus Christ as their Savior but also had to accept Adam as the Lord's chief prophet in order to obtain salvation. Likewise, in the days of Enoch, Noah, Abraham, and in every gospel dispensation, one must accept the Savior Jesus Christ and the prophet He chose to be His chief revealer and spokesman in that day. So it is today. To be saved in the celestial kingdom, we must accept Jesus Christ as the Savior and Joseph Smith as His Prophet.

At the beginning of this dispensation, the Lord declared to Joseph Smith, "This generation shall have my word through you" (D&C 5:10). This perfectly illustrates the dispensation concept and the role of a dispensation head. What this powerful statement means is that in our dispensation the Lord Jesus Christ has chosen Joseph Smith to be His chief revealer and spokesman. The Lord is saying, in effect, "If you want to know My words and be saved by My gospel in this day and age, then you must receive it through Joseph Smith. He is the one I have appointed to dispense and restore these things to the earth today." As a result, "We come to believe in Jesus Christ through the testimony of the Prophet Joseph Smith" (Dieter F. Uchtdorf, "The Fruits of the First Vision," 38).

Elaborating on this principle and specifically interpreting Doctrine and Covenants 5:10, Elder Bruce R. McConkie explained, "The generation of which we speak is this era or period of time. It is the dispensation in which we live; it is the time from the opening of our dispensation down to the second coming of the Son of Man; and for that allotted period of the earth's history, the word of the Lord, the word of salvation, the word of light and truth are going to the world *through Joseph Smith, and in no other way and through no one else*" ("'This Generation Shall Have My Word through You,'" 54; emphasis added).

Thus, in our day, the word of the Lord, the gospel of salvation, and the authority of the priesthood all trace themselves back to the Lord Jesus Christ *through* the Prophet Joseph Smith. We cannot receive these things from the Lord today independent of Joseph Smith, the dispensation head. "Through Joseph Smith have been restored all the powers, keys, teachings, and ordinances necessary for salvation and exaltation. You cannot go anywhere else in the world and get that. It is not to be found in any other church" (Tad R. Callister, "Joseph Smith—Prophet of the Restoration," 37).

A powerful illustration of this dispensation concept is seen in every man's priesthood line of authority. Because the priesthood was lost during the Great Apostasy and restored through Joseph Smith, there is no true priesthood authority on this earth except that which comes through the Prophet Joseph Smith. Even our living prophet presides over the Church today because he is the "authorized successor to Joseph Smith. He and the present apostles trace their authority to Jesus Christ in an unbroken chain of ordinations through Joseph Smith" (*Preach My Gospel*, 37). Every young man who holds the priesthood can test this principle by simply examining his priesthood line of authority; there, he will discover that the authority he has received comes from Jesus Christ *through* the Prophet Joseph Smith.

This principle not only applies to priesthood authority but also to gospel truth. As Elder M. Russell Ballard has explained, "Because of Joseph Smith, we have been given much. Were it not for the Restoration we would not know the true nature of God, our Heavenly Father, or our own divine nature as His children" and so many other important truths ("Creating a Gospel-Sharing Home," *Ensign*, May 2006, 84). As a result, we trace our knowledge of the gospel and plan of salvation *through* the Prophet Joseph Smith. It was through him that we received the Book of Mormon, which contains the "fulness of the gospel" (D&C 20:9). It was also through Joseph Smith that we continued to receive the word of the Lord through additional latter-day revelation found in the Doctrine and Covenants. Nearly every revelation found in that book begins with a section heading providing the same explanation—it is a "revelation given *through* Joseph Smith the Prophet." Truly, in our dispensation, the Lord has chosen to reveal His word through Joseph Smith (D&C 5:10).

President Marion G. Romney expounded on this point saying that

> It is a good thing for us to realize that we do not get the gospel of Jesus Christ out of the Bible only. . . .
>
> In each dispensation, from the days of Adam to the days of the Prophet Joseph Smith, the Lord has revealed anew the principles of the gospel. So that while the records of past dispensations, insofar as they are uncorrupted, testify to the truths of the gospel, still each dispensation has had revealed in its day sufficient truth to guide the people of the new dispensation, independent of the records of the past.
>
> I do not wish to discredit in any manner the records we have of the truths revealed by the Lord in past dispensations. What I now desire is to impress upon our minds that the gospel, as revealed to the Prophet Joseph Smith, is complete and is the word direct from heaven to this dispensation. It alone is sufficient to teach us the principles of eternal life. It is the truth revealed, the commandments given in this

dispensation through modern prophets by which we are to be governed. ("A Glorious Promise," *Ensign*, January 1981, 2)

This is why the Lord has always commanded us to teach about Joseph Smith in our missionary efforts. For example, in one of the earliest mission calls recorded in this dispensation, we find this profound instruction: "Lift up your heart and rejoice, for the hour of your mission is come; and your tongue shall be loosed, and you shall declare glad tidings of great joy unto this generation. *You shall declare the things which have been revealed to my servant, Joseph Smith* (D&C 31:3–4; emphasis added). Specifically, this mission call makes it clear that we are not called to declare the things revealed to Abraham, Moses, or Peter, even though they had the same gospel we do. It is a new dispensation, and the glad tidings and good news of our day is that God has spoken again to a modern prophet, and we are called to declare to the world what the Lord has revealed through Joseph Smith.

Even though the Prophet Joseph Smith died in 1844, he continues to be our dispensation head and the Prophet of the Restoration—"ever and ever the keys he will hold" ("Praise to the Man," *Hymns*, no. 27). The scriptures he has left us with continue to be the primary means by which we come to know the doctrines and principles of the gospel today. His successors, our living prophets and apostles, continue to testify of Joseph Smith, as well as explain and expand the revelations given to him by the authority he passed on to them. Therefore, to receive the gospel from living prophets and apostles today is to receive it *through* Joseph Smith. Truly, if anyone in all the world wants to know Christ and His gospel today, they must get it through Joseph Smith, and in no other way and through no one else.

Joseph Smith and Salvation

The implications of this doctrine are impressive, even provocative to some. As our article of faith declares, "We believe that through the Atonement of Christ, all mankind may be saved, by obedience to the laws and ordinances of the Gospel" (Articles of Faith 1:3). It is clear from this that salvation comes only through Jesus Christ, and that to be saved in the celestial kingdom we must obey the laws and ordinances of His gospel. Because Christ has restored these laws and ordinances through Joseph Smith, this means that Christ *requires us to receive Joseph*

Smith and the Restoration in order to be saved in the celestial kingdom of God.

Such a conclusion may seem dramatic to some, but this is exactly what the Lord Himself taught to the Nephites while He ministered among them. He prophesied that in the last days His word would be revealed in the Book of Mormon through the Prophet Joseph Smith. "Therefore it shall come to pass that whosoever will not believe in my words [the Book of Mormon], who am Jesus Christ, which the Father shall cause him [Joseph Smith] to bring forth unto the Gentiles . . . they shall be *cut off* from among my people (3 Nephi 21:11; emphasis added). "Cut off!" In other words, not saved. Jesus Christ Himself declared in this verse that those who reject the Book of Mormon as His word and Joseph Smith as His prophet will not be saved in the celestial kingdom of God, because to reject them is to reject Him. This is something every missionary must understand. No one can be truly and fully saved by Christ today without receiving Joseph Smith and the Book of Mormon.

Only when we understand this doctrine can we properly understand what President John Taylor meant when he said that "Joseph Smith, the Prophet and Seer of the Lord, has done more, save Jesus only, for the salvation of men in this world, than any other man that ever lived in it" (D&C 135:3). Jesus Christ and Joseph Smith work together to make salvation available to mankind today. Jesus Christ performed the work of atonement making salvation possible, and Joseph Smith performed the work of Restoration making salvation by Christ available. As a result, because of the work of Joseph Smith, we can be saved by Jesus Christ in our day because we have access to His restored gospel. In this work, Joseph Smith was not competing with Christ, as some mistakenly think. Rather, he was called of God to assist Jesus Christ in the work of salvation by restoring the gospel.

Jesus Christ and Joseph Smith

This is the concept of a dispensation head and this is the role of Joseph Smith, the Prophet of the Restoration—Christ administers salvation through him. "The work of the Prophet Joseph Smith is the Savior's work," said Elder Robert D. Hales ("Preparations for the Restoration and the Second Coming," *Ensign*, November 2005, 91). As a result, "we link the names of Jesus Christ and of Joseph Smith" in this dispensation and place them at the forefront of our message to the world (*Teachings of the Presidents of the Church: Joseph Fielding Smith*, 107).

To be saved in our day, we must gain a testimony of them both, and so must our investigators. Everyone must come to know that Jesus Christ is the Savior of mankind and that Joseph Smith is the Prophet of the Restoration. That is why we must never shy away from proclaiming the names of Jesus Christ and Joseph Smith. Not everyone will like this message, but Moroni warned us that the name of Joseph Smith "should be had for good and evil among all nations, kindreds, and tongues" (JS—H 1:33). If they accuse us of worshipping Joseph Smith, we respond by doing our best to help them understand and appreciate his role as Christ's chief latter-day prophet and revealer, but we never stop testifying of Joseph Smith. We do not want to be misunderstood, but we also do not want to abandon the message the Lord has commanded us to declare. So, in the face of opposition, we just keep teaching what the Lord has sent us to teach.

Remember, our missionary commission is to teach the *restored gospel*, which is "the gospel of Jesus Christ as restored through the Prophet *Joseph Smith*" (*Preach My Gospel*, 1). By teaching the *restored gospel*, we place the proper emphasis on both their roles and forever link the names of the Savior of the world and the Prophet of the Restoration in our testimonies to the world. This commission compels us to not teach investigators about Jesus Christ and His gospel independent of Joseph Smith and the Restoration. We must make it clear that if someone wants the gospel in our day, then they must get it as it is administered through the prophets of our day. They must get it through Joseph Smith.

As a teacher in the MTC, I remember wanting to impress this upon the minds of my missionaries. I wanted them to understand the complementary roles of Jesus Christ and Joseph Smith and why these two names are inseparably connected in the message of the restored gospel. One morning as I was flipping through the Book of Mormon searching for a devotional thought to share with them, my eye caught hold of something. At the front of the blue missionary copies of the Book of Mormon, there are several images. The first image in the book is that of the Savior Jesus Christ. I pondered the significance of that, understanding that its placement at the front of the book was symbolic of Christ being the primary message of the Book of Mormon and our message as missionaries. After thoughtfully considering the significance of the placement of that image, I flipped the page over and was deeply touched by what I saw on the back. The second image was that of Joseph Smith.

The thought I shared that day with my missionaries was this: Jesus Christ is our Savior; He comes first, and Joseph Smith is His latter-day Prophet, so he comes second (see D&C 135:3). Just as they are inseparably joined together on this page, so they are inseparably joined together in our message to the world. As they are the two sides of the same page, so they are the two sides of our message. And they are united as one. Try to separate them or pull them apart and it would destroy the message of them both, just as it would if you tried to tear them apart on this page. They stand together forever, and the Book of Mormon bears witness of them both. They combine to form the message of the *restored gospel*, which we have been called to declare.

May we never forget that lesson. The names of Jesus Christ and Joseph Smith go hand-in-hand. We cannot diminish the message of one without damaging the message of the other.

As President J. Reuben Clark expressed,

> There are for the Church and for each and all of its members two prime things which may not be overlooked, forgotten, shaded, or discarded:
>
> First—that Jesus Christ is the Son of God . . . that He was cruci-fied; that His spirit left His body; that He died; that He was laid away in the tomb; that on the third day His spirit was reunited with His body, which again became a living being; that He was raised from the tomb a resurrected being, a perfect Being. . . .
>
> The second of the two things to which we must all give full faith is that the Father and the Son actually and in truth and very deed appeared to the Prophet Joseph in a vision in the woods; that other heavenly visions followed to Joseph and to others; that the gospel and the Holy Priesthood, after the Order of the Son of God, were in truth and fact restored. . . .
>
> These facts . . . together with all things necessarily implied therein or flowing therefrom, must stand, unchanged, unmodified, without dilution, excuse, apology, or avoidance; they may not be explained away or submerged. Without these two great beliefs the Church would cease to be the Church. . . .
>
> They are the latitude and longitude of the actual location and position of the Church, both in this world and in eternity. ("The Charted Course of the Church in Education," August 8 1938)

9

NEW REVELATION FROM THE LIVING CHRIST

As an educational exercise and to prepare them to be good missionaries, I sometimes put my students on the spot and ask them to turn to another person in the class and answer the question, "Are Mormons Christian?" When I ask my seminary students this question, they quickly and intensely affirm our Christianity, often appealing to the name of our Church to prove that we believe in Christ. They state their convictions and even bear their testimonies that Jesus is the Christ, the Son of God and the Savior of the world. Most of them are then quite surprised when I tell them that most of those who accuse us of not being Christian do so with a full knowledge of the name of our Church and of our professed belief in Christ. This usually gets them thinking and compels them to ask a thoughtful question that we as missionaries must understand clearly: "So, why *do* so many Christians think that Mormons are not Christian?"

As Elder Jeffrey R. Holland explained, "By and large any controversy in this matter [of whether we are Christian] has swirled around two doctrinal issues—our view of the Godhead and our belief in the principle of continuing revelation leading to an open scriptural canon" ("The Only True God and Jesus Christ Whom He Hath Sent," *Ensign*

November 2007, 40). In other words, it is *because* of our doctrine related to Christ—*not* despite it—that many do not consider us to be Christian. We believe that Jesus Christ is a separate being from God the Father and we also believe that Jesus Christ has spoken again in our day to living prophets, providing additional scripture to the Bible. Because these doctrines are contrary to the creeds and teachings of traditional Christianity, many do not consider us to be "Christian." This means that if we are to really address the issue, we must do more than proclaim our belief in Christ; we must address our belief in modern revelation, living prophets, and additional scripture.

So, how *do* we respond to those who criticize us for our belief in modern revelation and additional scripture? As with so many things, we do it the way Jesus Christ did.

Jesus Christ began his earthly ministry as a missionary. In fact, he was always a missionary, always sharing the gospel with whoever would listen. And it is interesting to notice what his introductory message was. After His baptism, the scriptures state that "from that time Jesus began to preach, and to say, Repent: for the kingdom of heaven is at hand" (Matthew 4:17). That simple statement is the summary of what might be called the first lesson of His missionary lesson plan.

Unfortunately, because of the scriptural language, the main point is sometimes missed by the modern reader. In this verse, the "kingdom of Heaven" means the true Church, and the phrase "at hand" means has come (see Bible Dictionary, "Kingdom of Heaven" and Matthew 4:17, footnote d). Therefore, what Jesus Christ was announcing as His introductory message to the world was that the *true Church had been restored* and that everyone was invited to *repent and join it.* In other words, Jesus Christ was teaching the message of the restoration of the Church in His day as His first lesson, just like *Preach My Gospel* trains missionaries to do today. Jesus Christ set the example as a restoration-focused missionary and then invited all His missionaries, then and now, to follow Him (see JST Matthew 7:9; D&C 42:7).

The reason Christ preached a message of restoration was that His day, like ours, had been preceded by an apostasy. Though the priesthood and gospel had not been lost completely, the fulness of the gospel was not available at that time in Jerusalem until Christ restored it. This is shown by the ministry of John the Baptist, who held the Aaronic Priesthood and could baptize but repeatedly prophesied that what he offered was incomplete and that when Christ came, He would hold the Melchizedek Priesthood and thereby have the power to give the gift of the Holy Ghost (see Matthew 3:11, JS—H 1:70). When Christ came, not only did He restore the fulness of the priesthood, but He restored the fulness of the gospel in all its parts. He restored truths, ordinances, priesthood, and Church organization. In other words, Jesus Christ did in His day exactly what He called Joseph Smith to do in ours: He restored the fulness of the gospel. As a result, Jesus preached a very similar message in His day to what we preach in ours, a message of restoration centering on living prophets and new revelation.

An example of this is found in the famous Sermon on the Mount when Jesus Christ repeatedly introduced His topics by saying, "Ye have heard that it was said by them of old time . . ." (see Matthew 5:21, 27, 31, 33, 38, 43). Then, after rehearsing what had been said in the Old Testament, Christ would boldly announce, "But *I* say . . ." (see Matthew 5:22, 28, 32, 34, 39, 44; emphasis added). He then proceeded to provide new and additional instruction to the scriptures. What Jesus Christ was doing here is quite significant in terms of missionary work, and we must not miss the point. Those of "old time" that He was referring to were the prophets of the Old Testament like Moses, and what Jesus was doing was *adding* to their words. "*They* said that, but *I* say this." It is as if He were saying, "The prophets of old gave you the teachings of the Old Testament, but I give you the teachings of the New Testament." By doing so, Jesus presented new and additional revelation. He was *adding* to the scriptures. And who on earth has the right to do that? Only the living prophet, and Jesus Christ was the living prophet.

As a missionary, Jesus Christ boldly declared a message of restoration, of Himself as a living prophet, and of new revelation and additional scripture. And notice the reaction of the people at the end of the sermon: "And it came to pass, when Jesus had ended these sayings, the people were astonished at his doctrine: for he taught them as one having authority, and not as the scribes" (Matthew 7:28–29). They were "astonished." Why? Because He taught with power and authority. He sounded like something they had not heard in a very, very long time. He spoke like a living prophet, and what He offered them was new revelation and additional scripture.

Because Jesus Christ taught a message of restoration, emphasizing living prophets and new revelation, he was often criticized by the

Pharisees, a Jewish sect who couldn't handle the idea of new revelation. For them to accept new revelation was like putting "new wine into old bottles," Jesus declared, because it broke their apostate traditions and religious rules (Matthew 9:17). But the cunning Pharisees dodged the issue of their unwillingness to follow the living prophet and accept new revelation by trying to make it look like believing new revelation was somehow a threat or an insult to the old revelations written in their scriptures. Therefore, they constantly asserted their love of and loyalty to the scriptures of the past and accused Jesus and His disciples of not being true followers of former prophets like Moses and Abraham.

One example of this was when they told a man that had just been healed by Jesus Christ that, "Thou art his [Jesus's] disciple; but we are Moses' disciples. We know that God spoke unto Moses: as for this fellow [Jesus], we know not from whence he is" (John 9:29). By so declaring, they were rejecting the living prophet and new revelation while still claiming loyalty to dead prophets and the revelations of old.

Sound familiar? When we teach the same message today, we receive the same criticisms from the same type of people. This tactic of accusing those who accept living prophets and modern revelation of not following the prophets of old or believing the words of the Bible is actually not a new strategy. It was a common reaction of the Pharisees to Jesus and His followers.

The New Fulfills the Old

So how did Jesus respond? Jesus didn't respond by downplaying or denying new revelation, nor did He beg for their approval or clamor for their acceptance (like we sometimes mistakenly do today). Rather, Jesus responded by simply explaining the true relationship the new has with the old. Before he started adding to the scriptures in the Sermon on the Mount, He made a preliminary statement that should guide us in the way we present the concept of new revelation as missionaries. He said, "Think not that I am come to destroy the law, or the prophets: I am not come to destroy, but to fulfil" (Matthew 5:17). "The law" and "the prophets," as used here, refers to what we call the Old Testament (because it consisted primarily of the law of Moses and the words of the ancient prophets). To put this in our modern terminology, what the Lord is saying is, "Don't think that I have come to destroy the old revelations found in the Bible; living prophets and new revelation do not destroy the old, but rather fulfill it." And having said that, He proceeded to confidently add revelation and give additional scripture, found today in the New Testament.

Recognizing that we would face similar attacks in our day by those who would view new revelation as a threat to the old, the Lord counseled Joseph Smith to apply this same response to the new revelations of our day. Speaking specifically of the Book of Mormon, the Lord said, "Behold, I do not bring it to destroy that which they have received [in the Bible], but to build it up" (D&C 10:52). In saying this, Jesus Christ was paraphrasing what He said in the Sermon on the Mount, to again defend His own right to add to scripture.

This is the perfect example of how we should respond. This is how the Lord Himself responded and how He has specifically told us to respond. We don't avoid the issue of living prophets or downplay latter-day revelation, we do the opposite. We talk about them openly and directly. We don't run from the issue like cowards; we face it head on with courage. To those who accuse us of worshipping Joseph Smith or of not believing the Bible, we simply help them see that new revelation is not a threat to the old. The Book of Mormon does not destroy the Bible; rather, it "builds it up" by adding to it, clarifying its doctrines, fulfilling its prophecies, and supporting it with a confirming modern witnesses. Likewise, Joseph Smith's role does not threaten Jesus Christ, but rather it builds Him up by providing more of His words and restoring His gospel, thereby strengthening faith in Him (see D&C 1:21).

Our modern Apostles have followed this same pattern set forth by the Lord in responding to those who reject additional revelation and provide an example for us all. For example, Elder Russell M. Nelson has explained, "Love for the Book of Mormon expands one's love for the Bible and vice versa. Scriptures of the Restoration do not compete with the Bible; they complement the Bible" ("Scriptural Witnesses," *Ensign*, November 2007, 43). Similarly, Elder Jeffrey R. Holland has taught,

> Continuing revelation does not demean or discredit existing revelation. The Old Testament does not lose its value in our eyes when we are introduced to the New Testament, and the New Testament is only enhanced when we read the Book of Mormon: Another Testament of Jesus Christ. In considering the additional scripture accepted by Latter-day Saints, we might ask: Were those early Christians who for decades had access only to the primitive Gospel of Mark (generally

considered the first of the New Testament Gospels to be written)—
were they offended to receive the more detailed accounts set forth
later by Matthew and Luke, to say nothing of the unprecedented passages and revelatory emphasis offered later yet by John? Surely they
must have rejoiced that ever more convincing evidence of the divinity
of Christ kept coming. And so do we rejoice. ("'My Words . . . Never
Cease,'" 92)

The Book of Mormon is officially entitled "another" testament of
Jesus Christ, but it could just as accurately be titled a "new" testament
of Christ, because it is a new revelation of the gospel covenant for our
day (see D&C 84:57 and Jeffrey R. Holland, *Christ and the New Covenant*, 3–4). When we realize this, we see that the Book of Mormon and
other latter-day scriptures are for us today precisely what the teachings
of the New Testament were to those in that day—new and additional
scriptures intended to add to and confirm the scripture that already
exists. That is one reason why it is properly called the "New" Testament;
because it was new revelation in that day. But from our standpoint, both
the Old and New Testaments of the Bible are an "old" testament to us
and the "new" testament for us is the Book of Mormon and latter-day
revelation (see Bruce R. McConkie, "Book of Mormon Seminar," BYU
June 3, 1984). Just as the New Testament is not a threat to the Old
Testament, so the "new" testament of the Book of Mormon is not a
threat to the "old" testament of the Bible. They are meant to be together,
united as one (see 2 Nephi 3:12; Ezekiel 37:17).

The Old Supports the New

Such is the relationship that new revelation has to the old, but
what of the relationship of the old revelations to the new? Jesus commented on this also when He told the Pharisees to "search the scriptures" because "they are they which testify of me" (John 5:39). His point
was that the old revelations testify of Him and the new revelations He
declared. Continuing this thought, He said, "Do not think that I will
accuse you to the Father: there is one that accuseth you, even Moses, in
whom ye trust. For had ye believed Moses, ye would have believed me:
for he wrote of me. But if ye believe not his writings, how shall ye believe
my words?" (John 5:45–47). The Lord's reasoning here is both insightful and incriminating. Dead prophets support living prophets. The
old revelations testify and prophesy of the new revelations. Ultimately,

Jesus won't have to condemn the Jews who rejected Him; they will be condemned by their beloved prophet Moses, because Moses testified of Christ. Had they really believed Moses, they would have believed in Jesus Christ.

This principle has powerful application today. What Jesus was implying is that if you really believe the old revelations, then you will really believe the new revelations, because the old testifies of the new. If you really love the prophets of old, then you will really love the prophets of your day, because dead prophets direct us to follow the living prophets. To say it plainly, if you really love the Bible, then you will love the Book of Mormon. If you really love Peter and Paul, then you will love Joseph Smith and his successors. If you reject the living prophets and the new revelation of your day, what does that imply about your true feelings regarding the prophets and scripture of old?

This is a point the prophets of the Book of Mormon make very clear. For example, in Nephi's closing testimony, he boldly proclaimed, "Hearken unto these words and believe in Christ. . . . *And if ye shall believe in Christ ye will believe in these words, for they are the words of Christ*" (2 Nephi 33:10; emphasis added). In other words, those who truly believe in Christ will believe in and accept the Book of Mormon (see 2 Nephi 33 chapter heading). Mormon made a similar point in his own closing testimony when he stated that the Book of Mormon "is written for the intent that ye may believe [the Bible], and if ye believe [the Bible] ye will believe [the Book of Mormon] also" (Mormon 7:8–9; see also Mormon 7 chapter heading). The prophetic authors of the Book of Mormon were plain on this matter—all true believers of Christ and the Bible will also be led to believe the Book of Mormon.

And shouldn't that be obvious? Why would anyone who loves the word of God ever say, "We have received the word of God, and we need no more of the word of God, for we have enough" (2 Nephi 28:29)? Or, "A Bible! A Bible! We have got a Bible, and there cannot be any more Bible" (2 Nephi 29:3)? Why would anyone who really loves the Bible ever complain about receiving more of God's word (see 2 Nephi 29:8)? If your favorite author came out with a new book, wouldn't you be excited to read it? And would you ever think to protest against it?

The Old *and* the New

When we understand the true and proper relationship of new revelation to old revelation, we realize that no one is forced to choose between them. Do not be deceived; old revelation and new revelation are not in competition or conflict. They do not contradict. It is false to believe that you must either choose to believe the new or the old, because they are united as one, in perfect harmony, complementing and supporting each other. In fact, it is because we love the Bible that we love the Book of Mormon, because it adds to, clarifies, and unlocks it. And it is because we love Jesus Christ that we love Joseph Smith, for he is the revealer of Christ in our day. As mentioned earlier, "We don't ask any people to throw away any good they have got; we only ask them to come and get more" (*Teachings of the Prophet Joseph Smith*, 275).

This is exactly what we must help our investigators understand, that they don't have to choose between the new and the old, the living and the dead. They don't have to give up the Bible to believe the Book of Mormon. The new doesn't destroy the old; rather, it fulfills it, builds it up, clarifies, complements, and confirms it (see Matthew 5:17; D&C 10:52). To those who accuse us of not being Christian because of our belief in new revelation and additional scripture, we should simply respond that we believe in Christ and we believe in all that He has revealed, both the old and the new (see Articles of Faith 1:9).

When we understand the true and proper relationship of new revelation to old revelation, we begin to realize why our critics would try to make it appear that we must choose between them. By making it seem like new and old revelation are incompatible and opposed to each other, our critics have created what is called a false dichotomy. In other words, they try to force us to make a choice we don't have to make by presenting it as if there are only two options. By framing it as a choice between believing the Bible or the Book of Mormon, and Jesus Christ or Joseph Smith, they have set up a trap. If we choose Joseph Smith and the Book of Mormon, then we deny Christ and reject the Bible. On the other hand, if we choose Christ and the Bible, our critics may applaud our decision and embrace us as "Christian," but we will have denied the Restoration and betrayed our message. Either choice is unacceptable. Either way, we lose.

Unfortunately, we can too often fall right into this trap! Instead of proclaiming our belief in both the old *and* the new, we sometimes become defensive and spend our time affirming our belief in the Bible and in Jesus Christ while retreating from the message of the Book of Mormon and Joseph Smith. By focusing exclusively on the old revelations and ignoring the new ones, we are inadvertently accepting the assumption that we must choose between them, and we are falling right into the trap. It is time we finally recognize this trap and avoid it.

We do not have to choose between Jesus Christ and Joseph Smith, and when we do so, it only supports our critics' positions and diverts our attention from the message of the Restoration that Christ has called us to declare.

The *Living* Christ

So how do we make the point that we believe both without picking one and ignoring the other? When Jesus's critics came to Him claiming to believe in Jehovah and revere Abraham, notice how Jesus responded. He didn't accept the assumption that believing the old and believing the new are contradictory positions or that His disciples must either choose to believe the New Testament Jesus or the Old Testament Jehovah. Instead, He first explained that "Abraham rejoiced to see my day," and then boldly proclaimed, "I am" Jehovah (John 8:56, 58; see also footnote 58b and chapter heading).

This response is perfect. By it, Jesus Christ affirmed that living prophets and new revelation are not a threat to the old; rather, the old prophets like Abraham looked forward to Him and His day. Then, to show the unity between the old and the new, He boldly declared that *He is* Jehovah. This announcement makes it perfectly clear why no one has to choose between the old and the new—because the Old Testament Jehovah *is* the New Testament Jesus. This powerful response perfectly sidestepped the trap by refusing to choose between the old and the new. Instead, it brought it back to the real issue, *not* whether they would believe in Jehovah as He spoke anciently, but whether they would receive Him, the living Jehovah, as He spoke *in their day.*

So how can we apply this principle and respond like that today? What is the latter-day equivalent of Jesus announcing that He is Jehovah? How can we sidestep the trap of choosing between the old and the new and show that they are united and that we believe in them both? We do this today by proclaiming the *living Christ.* As mentioned earlier, the living Christ is the title we use today to proclaim that the same Jesus

Christ of the Bible still lives today and shows that He lives by speaking through modern revelation to His latter-day prophets.

At the start of the new millennium, the First Presidency and Quorum of the Twelve Apostles published their special witness of the Lord under the title of "The Living Christ." I have grown to greatly appreciate this inspired declaration, especially for the example it sets for us in sharing the gospel. Their testimony begins by explaining that Jesus was the "Jehovah of the Old Testament" and the "Messiah of the New," thus affirming our faith in the biblical Jesus. But the testimony does not end there; it goes on to witness that this same Jesus "appeared to the boy Joseph Smith," that "His priesthood and His Church have been restored," that "He lives," and that "He will someday return to the earth" ("The Living Christ," *Ensign*, April, 2000, 2–3). In declaring this testimony, the statement weaves together scriptures from the Bible and from latter-day revelation.

I believe this provides a perfect example for all of us as missionaries—we must proclaim the living Christ. We cannot be content with merely informing people that we believe in the biblical Jesus; we must also help them understand that Christ continues to speak and act today. He appeared to Joseph Smith in the First Vision, He revealed another testament in the Book of Mormon, and He continues to speak through living prophets and latter-day revelation. In other words, He lives! He is not dead, He has not retired, He has not quit on us. We believe that He speaks and acts today—this is exactly what we mean when we proclaim our witness of the living Christ.

By proclaiming the living Christ to the world, we do exactly what Jesus did when He proclaimed that He is Jehovah. We avoid the distracting defensiveness, cut straight to the heart of the matter, and refocus on the real issue—not whether we will believe in Jesus as He spoke anciently, but whether they will receive Him, the living Christ, as He speaks *today*.

Always the Message

The living Christ with His newly revealed word has always been the primary message of missionary work in every dispensation. It is the first thing missionaries are sent to teach. Adam and Eve taught their children that the Lord had spoken *in their day* and had promised to redeem them from the Fall (see Moses 5:10–12). Noah proclaimed to the people that the Lord had spoken again *in their day* and revealed that if they did not repent, He would destroy them with a flood (see Moses 8:17). When Peter and the New Testament Apostles preached the gospel, they began by explaining the ministry, Atonement, and Resurrection of Christ as it had occurred *in their day* (see Acts 2:31–33; 3:13–16; 4:10–12; 10:37–43).

We follow the same pattern by beginning with the First Vision, where the living Christ appeared to the Prophet Joseph Smith and spoke again *in our day*. In every dispensation, it is the same; just as the newspaper reports *current* news, so missionaries proclaim the current news about the living Christ in their day. The word *gospel* literally means "good news," and the good news that we proclaim is this: He lives! He speaks! And this is what He has said and done *in our day*.

A story that illustrates why the message of the living Christ is so instructive to those who want to understand our beliefs is found in the life of one of my friends. As a religious educator and local Church leader, he was asked to address a group of religious leaders of other faiths. They wanted to know what "Mormons" believe. He stood up and announced, "I can summarize everything we believe in one word." He then wrote the word *Christ* on the chalkboard. Of course, Christ is central to everything we believe, but that didn't really answer their question, and so my friend wisely continued, "But that is not what you really want to know," he said. "What you want to know is what sets my faith apart and makes my Church different from all the other churches who also believe in Christ. Again, I can summarize it in one word." He then wrote the word *revelation* on the chalkboard and taught that everything that sets us apart can be reduced to the principle of modern revelation.

As I have reflected on that profound response over the years, it has occurred to me that the two points my friend was making are perfectly expressed in the single concept of the living Christ, the Christ who speaks today by revelation. That is the concept that will help the world understand what we really believe.

It is the living Christ who we must introduce to all the world, because it is only the living Christ who can save them. Just as in Jesus's day it was no longer enough to believe in Jehovah as revealed in the Old Testament; to be saved, you had to accept the living Christ and His New Testament teachings. So it is in our day. It is no longer sufficient to believe in Christ as revealed through the Bible alone; to be saved today, we must accept the living Christ and His latter-day revelations. As missionaries, we must invite all to come unto the living Christ and be saved.

Our Unique Position: He Lives!

To illustrate how the doctrine of the living Christ sets us apart from all other Christian churches, President Harold B. Lee recounted the following story.

At the world's fair, Brother McAllister, president of the New York Stake, told us of an experience he had that probably defines the distinction that I am trying to make in this particular subject. He was on a plane coming back from a business assignment in St Louis, and his seatmate was a Catholic priest. As they flew toward New York and become acquainted with each other, each discovered the other's identity as to church relationships. As they talked about various things, the Catholic priest said, "Have you been out to the world's fair?"

"Yes," Brother McAllister said. "I am on the committee that helped to plan our pavilion out there."

"Well, have you visited our Catholic exhibit?"

And again, Brother McAllister said yes.

And the priest said, "Well, I have been to the fair and I have visited your exhibit. At the Catholic exhibit we have the dead Christ— the *Pieta*. But the Mormon Pavilion has the live Christ, or the living Christ."

And in that I think there is a distinguishing difference. ("The Place of the Living Prophet, Seer, and Revelator," Brigham Young University address, July 8, 1964)

Indeed, that is a distinguishing difference between The Church of Jesus Christ of Latter-day Saints and all other churches. While others believe, as we do, that Christ died for our sins and was resurrected, only we believe that Christ shows that He lives today by speaking through living prophets and modern revelation. "Do we as Latter-day Saints really understand and appreciate the strength of our position?" President Hinckley asked. "Among the religions of the world, it is unique and wonderful. . . . We declare without equivocation that God the Father and His Son, the Lord Jesus Christ, appeared in person to the boy Joseph Smith. . . . Our whole strength rests on the validity of that" (Gordon B. Hinckley, "The Marvelous Foundation of Our Faith," *Ensign*, November 2002, 78–79).

As missionaries, we must understand and appreciate the strength of our unique position and have the confidence that there are many who want to hear it. We are the only Christian church that proclaims the living Christ—we alone testify that Christ lives and speaks today by modern revelation to living prophets. Every true believing Christian should want to hear this! Every true believing Christian should want to *believe* this! If this is true, it is the greatest news in Christianity since Jesus Christ was resurrected (see Joseph F. Smith, *Gospel Doctrine*, 495). And it is true.

As we serve as missionaries, we must declare our witness of the living Christ. We must help the world understand that we are Christian *and* that we are different, that we believe the Bible *and* that we also believe in latter-day revelation and that no one has to choose between believing the old revelations and the new, between the prophets of the past and the prophets of our day. We can believe both. We make all of this clear when we proclaim the living Christ.

When we declare our witness of the living Christ, we go beyond merely informing others that we are Christian; we show them that we are the only Church in which Christ speaks today. To those who accuse us of believing in Joseph Smith and *not* Jesus Christ, who say that we believe the Book of Mormon but not the Bible, we respond with our witness of the living Christ. By proclaiming the living Christ, we turn their attacks around and make it clear that the question is not whether we believe in the biblical Jesus, but rather whether *they* will believe in the living Christ who speaks today.

May we all, as missionaries, raise our voices and join in echoing that great declaration from God the Father in the First Vision: "This is [His] Beloved Son. Hear Him! (JS—H 1:17). Hear Him speak today through living prophets; Hear him speak today through the Book of Mormon and latter-day revelation; Hear him speak today in this, His true and living Church. That is our message—He lives, and let us "Hear Him!" (JS—H 1:17)

> In declaring new scripture and continuing revelation, we pray we will never be arrogant or insensitive. But after a sacred vision in a now sacred grove answered in the affirmative the question "Does God exist?" what Joseph Smith and The Church of Jesus Christ of

Latter-day Saints force us to face is the next interrogative, which necessarily follows: "Does He speak?" We bring the good news that He does and that He has. With a love and affection born of our Christianity, we invite all to inquire into the wonder of what God has said since Biblical times and is saying even now. (Jeffrey R. Holland, "'My Words . . . Never Cease,'" 93)

10

OF GOD OR NOT OF GOD

Years ago, a program on television caught my attention. It was produced by a Christian outreach ministry, and the show's stated objective was to "save" erring "Mormons." I quickly discovered what Joseph Smith recognized so many years ago, that their "seemingly good feelings . . . were more pretended than real" (JS—H 1:6).

But one of the questions from a call-in listener intrigued me. She asked, "How do the Mormons get so many converts?" I thought that was a great question, and I was very curious about how the preacher would respond. What he said was intended to ridicule us, and yet it was surprisingly accurate. His explanation was that the reason so many "fall" for the message of those young missionaries is that they trust their "feelings" when they pray. This supposedly religious man then completely discounted the Lord's ability to communicate with us through inspired thoughts and feelings. Repeatedly, he used the word *feeling* with contempt, mocking the idea that God could speak to us in such a way—at one point he even attributed such feelings to heartburn from eating Mexican food! He concluded by counseling his listeners *not* to trust their feelings when they pray, but instead to trust the Bible, meaning his interpretation of the Bible.

I had to agree with his assessment. People *do* join the Church because they trust their feelings when they pray, and the most effective way to keep a person out of the Church *is* for them to ignore these feelings in favor of uninspired interpretations of the Bible. But what he failed to recognize—or at least refused to accept—is that these feelings are far more than mere emotions; they are inspired by the Lord and come as a manifestation of the spirit of revelation (see D&C 8:1–3). The Spirit of God often comes as a *feeling*, and that feeling often comes as an answer to prayer. It is true that this *is* how we get so many converts, because this is how God invites all to know for themselves. They must ask God.

Ask of God

There is nothing more fundamental in missionary work than the simple principle of asking God. "No message appears in scripture more times, in more ways than, 'Ask, and ye shall receive'" (Boyd K. Packer, "Reverence Invites Revelation, *Ensign*, November 1991, 21). Despite the prevalence of this invitation in the Bible, we are the only Church that I am aware of that invites our investigators to put that principle to practice in finding out which church is true. This not only demonstrates our belief in personal revelation but also the confidence we have in our message. It is one of the evidences that this Church is true, because who else has such faith in God and confidence in their message that they say, "Don't just take my word for it. Ask God, and He will tell you that what I have said is true"?

Settling the question of which church is true by asking God makes us unique as a church today, but there is really nothing new about this approach. It has been central to the missionary labors of Christ's true Church from the beginning. In fact, it was the counsel the Lord gave the original Twelve Apostles before sending them on their missions. After commissioning them to go forth and invite all to repent and join the newly restored Church, the Lord gave instruction about how they might establish their converts on the foundation of personal testimony. He counseled His missionaries to "say unto them, Ask of God" (JST Matthew 7:12).

The parallels between missionary work in the New Testament and in our day are striking. Not only did they teach a message of restoration like we teach today, but they also extended the same invitation to investigators that we extend today. They invited them to find out for themselves by asking God. "Ask, and it shall be given you; seek, and ye shall find; knock, and it shall be opened unto you. For everyone that asketh, receiveth; and he that seeketh, findeth; and unto him that knocketh, it shall be opened" (JST Matthew 7:12–13). Interestingly, they also received the same objections by those who claimed that God no longer spoke like he did in the days of Moses and that the old revelations and scriptures were sufficient (see JST Matthew 7:9–15). From dispensation to dispensation, the fundamentals of missionary work do not change. All must gain a testimony for themselves; therefore, all must ask of God.

This pattern of asking God in faith and receiving an answer by the Spirit is the means by which each of us can know for ourselves that these things are true. Like Joseph Smith, we are not expected to simply place our trust in mankind's limited wisdom because it is "impossible for [mankind] . . . to come to any certain conclusion who was right and who was wrong" (JS—H 1:8). Nor are we to blindly trust the man-made interpretations from those who "[understand] the same passages of scripture so differently as to destroy all confidence in settling the question by an appeal to the Bible"; we must get "wisdom from God" by *asking of God* (JS—H 1:12). Only God can give us that testimony, that sure spiritual witness that man cannot give or take away (see JS—H 1:23–24). Only then can we truly know for ourselves. As stated in *Preach My Gospel*, "No one can know of spiritual truths without prayer" (*Preach My Gospel*, 39). Like Joseph Smith, we "must either remain in darkness and confusion, or else [we] must . . . ask of God" (JS—H 1:13).

Ask God. That simple, powerful, perfect invitation is our response to all who seek to know for themselves if this message is true. They must ask God, not as an isolated event, but as part of the process of diligent searching and faithful working. They must ask Him in sincerity and faith, believing that He will answer by the power of the Holy Ghost. In every dispensation, this principle is constant and the invitation remains the same: "If any of you lack wisdom, let him ask of God" (James 1:5). "That's our message: 'Ask God.' . . . The Restoration began with Joseph Smith on his knees in the Sacred Grove and that is where the testimony of every Latter-day Saint must begin, on their knees in a sacred moment asking of God" (Joseph Fielding McConkie, "The First Vision and Religious Tolerance" in *A Witness for the Restoration*, 177–99).

Knowing the Things of God

The reason why we must ask of God is because the only way to know spiritual truths is by the Spirit of the Holy Ghost. This is a point the scriptures and latter-day prophets have made unmistakably clear. For example, consider the following scriptures: "The things of God knoweth no man, except he has the Spirit of God" (JST 1 Corinthians 2:11), and "no man knoweth of [God's] ways save it be revealed unto him" (Jacob 4:8). Joseph Smith further explained that "no man can know that Jesus is the Lord, but by the Holy Ghost," "we never can comprehend the things of God and of heaven but by revelation," and "the things of God [are] known only by the Spirit of God" (*Teachings of the Prophet Joseph Smith*, 223, 292, 246).

Clearly, the only way to know the things of God is by the Spirit of God, and the most effective way to get that spiritual confirmation and witness is to ask of God—which brings us back to the story at the start of this chapter. The reason why this minister mocked the idea of asking God and receiving revelation through inspired feelings was because "the natural man receiveth not the things of the Spirit of God: *for they are foolishness unto him*: neither can he know them, because they are spiritually discerned" (1 Corinthians 2:14; emphasis added). Inspired feelings were foolishness to this minister because he was what the scriptures call a natural man. He did not understand spiritual things because he did not have the Spirit. Despite his claims, he had not been born again.

To understand the situation, perhaps it might be helpful to view all things as either belonging to the natural world or the spiritual world. Because the things of the natural world are physical in nature, they can be quantitatively measured and empirically observed; they can be seen with the natural eyes and heard by the natural ears; they can be learned and known by the powers of reason and by the faculties of the five senses. On the other hand, the spiritual world includes the things of God—spiritual things, like the existence of God—which cannot be readily observed by the natural senses because they do not belong to the natural world. They lie beyond the veil, and so the only way to know them is by communication from beyond the veil. This communication comes by the Spirit of the Holy Ghost, which is why spiritual things can only be learned and known by the Spirit (see JST 1 Corinthians 2:9–11).

To illustrate, consider a science teacher in the classroom. The Spirit would not need to be there to confirm the law of gravity to her students because they can visually observe it. To demonstrate it, all the teacher would need to do is drop her marker, and all of the students could watch it fall.

But gospel laws and truths are not so easily observed. For example, to learn about the law of repentance, I couldn't invite a student to the front of class and say, "Watch what happens when he repents!" Likewise, I couldn't invite my students to be in the Sacred Grove and observe the First Vision. Because these things are spiritual in nature, the only way to really know that they are true is for the Spirit to confirm that truth to us in our hearts. They are beyond the natural world, and so they can never be proved or disproved using only the natural senses.

"There is a natural world and there is a spiritual world," said President J. Reuben Clarke, and "the things of the natural world will not explain the things of the spiritual world" ("The Charted Course of the Church in Education"). Ultimately, spiritual things can only be known by spiritual means, which is why the natural man will never know the things of God. They do not know the Spirit or trust spiritual feelings, so they are limited to the natural world for their knowledge and understanding. As a result, they must rely exclusively on their five natural senses and on their own powers of reason for all that they know and believe. The truths of the gospel will always be a mystery and foolishness to such a person because they are spiritually blind to them and cannot understand them (see 1 Corinthians 2:14).

Elder Dallin H. Oaks explained this when he stated, "Those who rely exclusively on study and reason reject or remain doubtful of all absolutes that cannot be established through the five senses, including good and evil and the existence and omniscience of God. They also reject all other methods of acquiring knowledge, including revelation (Oaks, *The Lord's Way* [Salt Lake City: Deseret Book, 1991], 52). Because of this self-imposed natural limitation, they can never know the spiritual things of God, which is why President Boyd K. Packer has repeatedly declared, "If all you know is what you see with your natural eyes and hear with your natural ears, then you will not know very much" (as quoted by David A. Bednar, "Quick to Observe," *Ensign*, December 2006, 36).

It is important to recognize that the Lord established these laws of how we can know spiritual things and he has done it on purpose. His plan is a plan of faith. By limiting the knowledge of spiritual things in this way, "one thing [is] for sure, the skeptic will never know, for he will not meet the requirement of faith, humility, and obedience to qualify him for the visitation of the Spirit. Can you not see that there is where testimony is hidden, protected from the perfectly insincere, from the intellectual, from the mere experimenter, the arrogant, the faithless, the proud? It will not come to them" (Boyd K. Packer, "The Candle of the Lord," *Ensign*, January 1983, 55).

Not of God

Often, however, because the natural man and woman refuse to rely on spiritual methods, they demand to know spiritual things on their own natural terms. Instead of learning that the gospel is true by the Spirit, they want to know in "some other way"; they seek a witness that is "not of God," but of mankind (D&C 50:20). They put their trust in man and in the "arm of flesh," rather than trusting in God and His Spirit to reveal these things (2 Nephi 4:34; 28:31). They demand natural, physical evidence and reasoning for spiritual things before they will believe.

The classic Book of Mormon example of this was Korihor, whose motto was this: "Ye cannot know of things which ye do not see" (Alma 30:15). Because he was a natural man, he would only accept what a natural man could witness and experience. He completely disregarded those inspired thoughts and feelings that come from the spirit of revelation, calling them "the effect of a frenzied mind" (Alma 30:16). Ultimately, he demanded natural, physical evidence for spiritual things, claiming, "If thou wilt show me a sign . . . then will I be convinced" (Alma 30:43). Of course, when he received a sign, he was not converted by it (see Alma 30:50–60). They never are.

Unfortunately, some missionaries are more than willing to accommodate the natural man by trying to provide non-spiritual evidence for our message. They attempt to prove the Church true to the natural man independent of the Spirit, relying on things like archeological evidence of the Book of Mormon or intellectual reasoning from the Bible. They seem to think, *If only I can get my investigators a man-made testimony, then they can transition to a God-given one.* This of course does not really work because, as the scriptures repeatedly state in word and demonstrate by experience, "faith cometh not by signs, but signs follow those that believe" (D&C 63:9).

Elder M. Russell Ballard explained this concept well when he was asked about scientific proof authenticating the Book of Mormon. He said,

> I don't believe that's how people will ever come to know whether or not the Book of Mormon is the word of God. I remember an experience that I had as mission president some years ago when I presided over the affairs of the Church in Eastern Canada. I met with about thirty different ministers of different religions and then I let them ask me questions and the very first question I was asked was by a fine minister who said, "Mr. Ballard, if you just give us the gold plates and let us see that they exist, then we would know that the Book of Mormon is true." And I looked at him and I said, "Father, you know better than that. You're a man of the cloth. You know that God has never revealed religious truth to the heart and soul of a man or a woman except by the power of the Spirit. Now you could have those plates, you could turn the pages, you could look at it, you could hold it, and you wouldn't know any more after that experience whether or not the book is true than you would have before. My question to you; have you ever read the Book of Mormon?" And he said, "No, I haven't." That's how people will come to know whether or not the Book of Mormon is true. You will not get to know it by trying to prove it archeologically or by DNA or by anything else in my judgment. Just pick it up and read it and pray about it and you will come to know religious truth is always confirmed by what you feel and that's the way Heavenly Father answers prayers. (Transcript of interview with Elder M. Russell Ballard, Mormon Newsroom, October 2, 2007)

This is a powerful insight that all of us should understand in sharing the gospel. We don't come to know spiritual things through scientific evidence or physical proofs. Seeing the gold plates would only prove that there were gold plates. Even if you could indisputably prove by archeology that a people called the Nephites lived in America and kept a record of their beliefs, that still wouldn't prove their beliefs were true. Spiritual things can only be known and proven by spiritual means and, as the Lord explained, those who won't believe the Book of Mormon based on the message it contains would not believe it even if they saw the gold plates (see D&C 5:7).

The same principle is true for the Bible. Archeology can prove that there was a Red Sea, but cannot prove that Moses parted it by the power of God. History can demonstrate that there was a man named Jesus that died in Jerusalem but cannot prove that He was the Son of God and that He rose from the dead. Just as you can't handle the gold plates of the Book of Mormon, you also can't handle the original manuscripts of the Bible. But even if you could, it would not prove that the Bible is true. "Scientific methods will not yield spiritual knowledge" (Dallin H. Oaks, "Testimony," *Ensign*, May 2008, 26). These are things that simply must be accepted on faith and can only be proven by the Spirit. Nothing else will do. Certainly there is a place for good scholarship in history and archeology, but the findings of which belong in academic dialogue, *not* in missionary discussions.

It is not that spiritual things are unreasonable, unintelligible, or incomprehensible, or that there is no physical evidence for spiritual things like the Book of Mormon, but these tools alone are insufficient in gaining the spiritual witness we need. As Elder Bruce R. McConkie explained, "Intellectual things—reason and logic—can do some good, and they can prepare the way, and they can get the mind ready to receive the Spirit under certain circumstances. But conversion comes and the truth sinks into the hearts of people only when it is taught by the power of the Spirit" (Bruce R. McConkie, *Sermons and Writings* [Salt Lake City: Bookcraft, 1989], 332).

Physical or intellectual evidence may *convince* a person for a time that the Church is true, but our goal is not just to convince them to join the church, but rather to *convert* them to the restored gospel so they will endure to the end. Because conversion cannot happen without the Spirit, nothing short of a true spiritual witness will ever do. As President Brigham Young observed,

> I had only traveled a short time to testify to the people, before I learned this one fact, that you might prove doctrine from the Bible till doomsday, and it would merely convince a people, but would not convert them. You might read the Bible from Genesis to Revelation, and prove every iota that you advance, and that alone would have no converting influence upon the people. Nothing short of a testimony by the power of the Holy Ghost would bring light and knowledge to them—bring them in their hearts to repentance. Nothing short of

that would ever do." (Brigham Young, *Journal of Discourses* [London: Latter-day Saints' Book Depot, 1854–86], 5:327)

As the Lord explained to Peter, true testimony must come not by "flesh and blood," meaning physical evidence or intellectual reasoning; it must be revealed by our Father in Heaven through His Holy Spirit (Matthew 16:16–17). There is no substitute for the Holy Ghost. Whatever efforts we make to convince others with reasoned arguments from the Bible, or archeological evidence for the Book of Mormon, or any other man-made sources of testimony will be fleeting and short-lived. It will not give them an enduring conversion to the restored gospel. Only when they are built upon the rock of spiritual testimony will they be protected and preserved. All those who are built on the sandy foundation of man-made testimony will be washed away when the storms of life come (see Matthew 7:24–27, Helaman 5:12). We all know examples of those who have left the Church because their testimonies were based on intellectual evidence rather than on a spiritual witness, and these weak testimonies did not endure the test of time and the trials of life (see *Selected Writings of Robert L. Millet*, 401–402).

Hearing the Voice of God

Of course, this simple, spiritual approach to sharing the gospel will not convince everyone. Thankfully, convincing everyone was never our job as missionaries. Not even Jesus convinced everyone, despite His many miracles and signs. Our job, like His, is *not* to convince the world but to find and gather the honest in heart, those "who are only kept from the truth because they know not where to find it" (D&C 123:12). Jesus made a promise about this that we need to remember: when sharing the gospel, "My sheep hear my voice, . . . and they follow me" (John 10:27). When missionaries simply teach the restored gospel by the Spirit, their voices are His voice, and His sheep will recognize and follow it (see D&C 1:4, 88:66). They won't need to be compelled or convinced; true sheep will hear and follow. As missionaries, we need to focus on gathering sheep, not convincing goats.

The Lord explained how this process works. He taught that there is a spiritual influence called the Light of Christ that "giveth light to every man that cometh into the world" (D&C 84:46). One purpose of this light is to lead and guide all of our Heavenly Father's children in this world of sin and darkness so that we can find our way back to Him. In this way, it is like an internal spiritual compass given to everyone to help us choose right from wrong and, if we follow it, will ultimately "lead the honest soul who 'hearkeneth to the voice' to find the true gospel and the true Church" (Bible Dictionary, "Light of Christ"; see also D&C 84:46–47 and *Preach My Gospel*, 90). Unfortunately, not everyone follows the Light of Christ and, as the Lord explained, whoever does not listen to and follow this light "is not acquainted with my voice, and is not of me" (D&C 84:52). That is to say, they are not His sheep because they do not hearken to and follow His voice as He speaks to them through the Light of Christ.

When properly understood, this is a liberating doctrine for missionaries. It means that everyone on earth is given enough of the Light of Christ to find the true Church if they will follow it. It also means that if someone doesn't recognize the true Church when they learn of it, it is because they have not been following the Light of Christ that they were born with. In other words, it's their own fault. This lifts the burden of salvation off the missionary and places it squarely on the shoulders of the investigator. They are responsible for their own salvation. It is not our job to convince them; our job is simply to teach and to testify, and it is their job to be spiritually prepared enough to recognize the truth when they hear it. This is comforting to those of us who try to share the restored gospel but are worried that we might not know enough or speak eloquently enough because, as one friend and colleague observed, "If they're ready, it doesn't really matter what you say. And if they're not ready, it doesn't really matter what you say."

When the honest in heart hear the restored gospel, they *feel* something and they know what they are hearing is true. This is what Joseph Smith meant when he explained, "This is good doctrine. *It tastes good.* I can taste the principles of eternal life, and so can you . . . *you taste them,* and I know that *you believe them* . . . [and] you are bound to receive them as sweet, and rejoice more and more" (*Teachings of the Prophet Joseph Smith*, 355; emphasis added). When gospel truth is taught by the Spirit, "it tastes good," or in other words it feels right (see D&C 9:8). This feeling causes the honest in heart to believe it and makes them bound to receive it as truth. For the honest in heart, "truth carries its own influence and recommends itself" (Andrew F. Ehat, *Words of Joseph Smith* [Provo, Utah: Grandin Book, 1991], 237); it "has within itself the evidence of its own authenticity" (Marion G. Romney, "The Way of Life," *Ensign*, May 1976, 81).

This principle is especially true of "the key messages of the Restoration," which, President Dieter F. Uchtdorf explained, "have the power to bring divine feelings to the heart and mind of the earnest seeker of truth" ("Truth Restored," BYU Speeches, August 22, 2006). We don't need to feel like we have to compel or force or manipulate or convince others to believe our message because, for the honest in heart, it will be convincing enough on its own. As Joseph Smith taught, "I will not seek to compel any man to believe as I do, only by the force of reasoning, for truth will cut its own way" (*Teachings of the Prophet Joseph Smith*, 313). In other words, when the gospel is taught right, the Spirit does the work of convincing and proving for us. His sheep will hear His voice and follow Him.

The Power of God

The Lord's instruction to all of us is simple. We are to "preach [His] gospel by the Spirit" (D&C 50:14). That simple sentence summarizes our responsibility in sharing the gospel (as evidenced by the fact that the current missionary lesson guide borrows its title from that phrase). From it, we learn *what* we should teach and *how* we should teach it, and then we are told emphatically that if we do it in "some other way it is *not of God*" (D&C 50:18; emphasis added). We don't need to worry about being experts on the Bible or on archeological evidence of the Book of Mormon or on any of the other things we sometimes think we need to know to effectively share the gospel. We simply need to have a knowledge and testimony of the restored gospel and a willingness to share it. Then we step back and let the Spirit do the work in missionary work.

The Apostle Paul is a perfect example of a missionary who knew and understood this simple commission and recognized that it was the source of his great missionary success. He explained to the Corinthian Saints, "And I, brethren, when I came to you, came not with excellency of speech or of wisdom, declaring unto you the testimony of God. For I determined not to know any thing among you, save Jesus Christ, and him crucified. . . . And my speech and my preaching was not with enticing words of man's wisdom, but in demonstration of the Spirit and of power" (1 Corinthians 2:1–2, 4).

When Paul preached, he didn't teach "any thing . . . [except] Jesus Christ, and him crucified," meaning he only taught the basic principles of the gospel of Jesus Christ as they had had been revealed in his day (just as missionaries are trained to do today). He did not teach archeology or science or mingle his message with the philosophies of men. Nor did he rely on "excellency of speech" by using impressive and "enticing words" or relying on scientific evidence or "man's wisdom" and reasoning to prove his message true. He didn't try to counterfeit the Spirit by emotional manipulation or intellectual reasoning. Rather, Paul simply declared the testimony he had received "of God," relying on God's Spirit and power to prove the truth of what he taught (1 Corinthians 2:1–2, 4). Paul taught the gospel by the Spirit, and he did this so that the testimonies and faith of his investigators "should not stand in the wisdom of men, but in the power of God" (1 Corinthians 2:5).

That simple pattern of preaching the gospel by the Spirit may not seem very impressive at first. To the world and the worldly, it appears foolish, but it is by this "foolishness of preaching" that God saves "them that believe" (1 Corinthians 1:21). This is perfectly illustrated in the conversion story of President Brigham Young.

> If all the talent, tact, wisdom, and refinement of the world had been sent to me with the Book of Mormon, and had declared, in the most exalted of earthly eloquence, the truth of it, undertaking to prove it by learning and worldly wisdom, they would have been to me like smoke which arises only to vanish away. But when I saw a man without eloquence or talents for public speaking, who could only say, "I know by the power of the Holy Ghost that the Book of Mormon is true, that Joseph Smith is a Prophet of the Lord," the Holy Ghost proceeding from that individual illuminated my understanding, and a light, glory, and immortality were before me. I was encircled by them, filled with them, and I knew for myself that the testimony of the man was true. (*Journal of Discourses* 1:90; quoted in *Preach My Gospel*, 199)

Elder Bruce R. McConkie explained this simple, spiritual pattern in these words:

> We are sent out to teach and to testify. Now, the reason we teach is so there will be a background, a foundation, a basis, to enable people to have an intelligent opinion when we bear testimony. . . . Conversion

comes when spirit speaks to spirit. If you teach the gospel, and get the right climate arranged, and then bear testimony that what you are saying is true, it strikes a responsive chord in the heart of the hearer . . . [and] his soul vibrates and responds to what you have said. He can't explain it, and he doesn't know why, but all of a sudden he knows that the work is true. We have got to do more testifying. (Bruce R. McConkie, "Seven Steps to More and Better Converts," Mission Presidents' Seminar, June 21, 1975)

Which brings me back to the story I shared at the beginning of this chapter. Why do we have so many converts? Because we invite all to ask of God, relying on His Spirit to prove His message true. This is something that the natural man will never understand. Which is why the preacher mentioned earlier not only mocked the spirit of revelation but actually counseled his listeners not to ask God, but rather just to trust him and his opinions about God instead. The natural man will always prefer the reasoning of men over the revelations of God. They will always prefer physical evidence to spiritual proof. As a result, they will never know the things of God and they will always be confused by why so many people join the true Church of Jesus Christ.

11

LOYAL TO THE RESTORATION

There is a classic story that illustrates the main message of this chapter and a central theme of this book. It is a story that was often told by President David O. McKay to missionaries to show how his father learned the hard way that we should be loyal to the Restoration. He related,

> When [my father] began preaching in his native land and bore testimony of the restoration of the gospel of Jesus Christ, he noticed that the people turned away from him. They were bitter in their hearts against anything [related to the Church], and the name of Joseph Smith seemed to arouse antagonism in their hearts. One day he concluded that the best way to reach these people would be to preach just the simple principles, the atonement of the Lord Jesus Christ, the first principles of the gospel, and not bear testimony of the restoration. In a month or so he became oppressed with a gloomy, downcast feeling, and he could not enter into the spirit of his work. He did not really know what was the matter, but his mind became obstructed; his spirit became depressed; he was oppressed and hampered; and that feeling of depression continued until it weighed him down with such heaviness that he went to the Lord and said: "Unless I can get this feeling

removed, I shall have to go home. I can't continue having my work thus hampered."

The discouragement continued for some time after that, when, one morning before daylight, following a sleepless night, he decided to retire to a cave, near the ocean, where he knew he would be shut off from the world entirely, and there pour out his soul to God and ask why he was oppressed with this feeling, what he had done, and what he could do to throw it off and continue his work. He started out in the dark toward the cave. He became so eager to get to it that he started to run. As he was leaving the town, he was hailed by an officer who wanted to know what was the matter. He gave some noncommittal but satisfactory reply and was permitted to go on. Something just seemed to drive him; he had to get relief. He entered the cave or sheltered opening, and said, "Oh, Father, what can I do to have this feeling removed? I must have it lifted or I cannot continue in this work"; and he heard a voice, as distinct as the tone I am now uttering, say, "Testify that Joseph Smith is a prophet of God." Remembering then what he tacitly had decided six weeks or more before, and becoming overwhelmed with the thought, the whole thing came to him in a realization that he was there for a special mission, and he had not given that special mission the attention it deserved. Then he cried in his heart, "Lord, it is enough," and went out from the cave. (*Teachings of Presidents of the Church: David O. McKay* [Salt Lake City: The Church of Jesus Christ of Latter-day Saints, 2011], 91–92)

This story perfectly illustrates one of our problems in sharing the gospel. Inevitably, when we are true to our commission to teach the restored gospel, false accusations will come from our critics who seek to justify their rejection of our message. Some will say that we worship Joseph Smith, that we are not Christian, or that we don't believe the Bible. As this story above demonstrates, there is a temptation to respond to this by avoiding the message of the Restoration and focusing instead on seeking "common ground," or "building on common beliefs." This often means focusing on doctrinal and religious points we have in common with other faiths while avoiding the differences that come from the Restoration. Typically, this is done by emphasizing Christ and His teachings in the New Testament while dismissing modern prophets like Joseph Smith and latter-day revelation like the Book of Mormon. This effort to avoid the restored gospel is done in attempt to assure everyone that we are just like them, or at least similar enough like them to avoid their criticism.

As appealing as this approach might *sound* to some, it is contrary to our missionary commission to teach the restored gospel. In fact, avoiding Joseph Smith and the Restoration goes against everything God has called us to teach as missionaries. As President McKay reminded us, we have a "special mission" as missionaries. We are sent to teach the unique and distinctive beliefs of the Restoration, *not* just talk about the common beliefs we share with the world. President McKay's father learned a lesson the hard way that none of us should ever forget— when we fail to teach the Restoration, we fail as missionaries. When we neglect the special message we have been sent to declare, not only are we weak and ineffective, but we also offend God and come under condemnation. We cannot abandon Joseph Smith and discard the Book of Mormon with impunity. The lesson we must learn is to be loyal to the Restoration.

Offending God and Coming under Condemnation

One missionary who was clearly opposed to the practice of avoiding the Restoration in favor of emphasizing "common beliefs" was the Prophet Joseph Smith. From his great missionary example, we learn a powerful lesson for why we should be loyal to the Restoration. Elder Joseph B. Wirthlin related,

> In 1839 the Prophet Joseph Smith and several other Church leaders had the opportunity to address a congregation of 3,000 people in Philadelphia who were not members of the Church. Sidney Rigdon spoke first. *Attempting to establish common ground*, he taught the gospel by referring to the Bible and its prophecies. When Joseph arose to speak, he was displeased. He said that if others did not have the courage to testify of him, then he would testify of himself and of the Book of Mormon. Because of his speech, many were touched by the Spirit and were baptized into the Church. ("The Book of Mormon: The Heart of Missionary Proselyting," 13–14, emphasis added)

More on this remarkable story will be shared later in the chapter. For our purposes now, it is important to notice that this attempt to establish common ground by exclusively relying on the Bible upset the Prophet Joseph and that he did not shy away from teaching the very thing that Sidney Rigdon deliberately avoided—the Restoration of the gospel. Joseph Smith had the courage to testify of living prophets and latter-day revelation. He recognized what too many missionaries like Sidney Rigdon don't seem to understand, that excessively focusing on common beliefs too often means neglecting the message of the Restoration. To Joseph Smith, avoiding these truths was just a subtle way of denying them, and he would not deny the Restoration.

Remember, it was Joseph Smith who summarized his feelings about the First Vision with these words: "I had seen a vision; I knew it, and I knew that God knew it, and I could not deny it, neither dared I do it; at least I knew that by so doing I would offend God, and come under condemnation" (JS—H 1:25). Joseph Smith understood clearly that denying his testimony of the First Vision would offend God and bring him under condemnation. What he also understood was that denying one's testimony is not limited to the specific act of saying it's not true. According to the dictionary, denying also includes refusing to admit something is true. In other words, it would have been a denial of his testimony if Joseph Smith refused to openly declare it. As this story illustrates, Joseph Smith recognized his responsibility to actively testify of the Restoration and was bothered by those who refused to do the same.

What we must ask ourselves is this: To what degree are we under the same obligation as Joseph Smith to actively bear our own witness of the Restoration, no matter what the cost? If we refuse to bear that witness, don't we also "offend God, and come under condemnation" (JS—H 1:25)? Some avoid the message of the Restoration because they are too embarrassed to stand out and be different or too afraid of the criticism and persecution that might come from declaring it, but isn't avoiding the Restoration like a subtle way of denying it? Joseph Smith was never embarrassed to testify of the restored gospel, and we shouldn't be either. He risked his life to tell the story of the First Vision (JS—H 1:24–25); all we risk is our social acceptance. Can't we at least stand that tall? Those who neglect the message of the Restoration because they fear offending man need to remember that by so doing they risk offending God.

Unfortunately, these stories are not unusual in missionary work. Many have made the mistake of avoiding the Restoration and latter-day revelation in an effort to focus on "common beliefs" from the Bible. In the early days of the Church, enough missionaries were guilty of this practice that the Lord warned that the whole Church was under condemnation for it. Speaking to newly returned missionaries, the Lord said, "Your minds in times past have been darkened because of unbelief, and because you have treated lightly the things you have received [that is, the Book of Mormon and other scriptures and revelations of the Restoration]—which vanity and unbelief have brought the whole church under condemnation" (D&C 84:54–55).

Because missionaries had neglected the Restoration and latter-day revelation in missionary work, they had lost the Spirit and brought the whole Church under condemnation. President Ezra Taft Benson was concerned that we had still not fully learned that lesson as a church and therefore were still under that condemnation (see *A Witness and Warning*, 6–7, 17).

Coming Out from under Condemnation

For any still under this condemnation, the solution is simple—we must repent. The Lord explained to these early missionaries that the Church "shall remain under this condemnation until they repent and remember the new covenant, even the Book of Mormon and the former commandments [Doctrine and Covenants] which I have given them" (D&C 84:57). As the Lord explained, we repent of this sin by relying on the Book of Mormon and other latter-day revelations. This promise is elaborated a few verses later when the Lord explained, "I will forgive you of your sins [of neglecting the Restoration and latter-day revelation] with this commandment—that you remain steadfast in your minds in solemnity and the spirit of prayer, in bearing testimony to all the world of those things which are communicated unto you [revealed through the Restoration]" (D&C 84:61).

The message is clear. If neglecting the Restoration in missionary work got us into this trouble, then testifying of it will get us out. Only when we remember to teach and testify of the Book of Mormon and the other scriptures and revelations of the Restoration—"those things which are communicated unto [us]"—will we be free of this condemnation and have the success that we seek.

Despite these warnings of the past, this is a lesson we have been slow to learn as a church. Several decades ago, Elder Bruce R. McConkie made this observation to BYU religion professors: "Maybe in our efforts as a Church to ensure that everyone knows we're Christian, we have gone too far. A while back we changed our missionary discussions to make our first discussion a message about Christ. It seemed at the time a good thing to do, given that Jesus is the Head of the Church. But what was the result? A decrease in convert baptisms and a decrease in the number of copies of the Book of Mormon placed by full-time missionaries from one million per year to 500,000. We are not teaching the Restoration as we ought to" (Joseph Fielding McConkie, *The Bruce R. McConkie Story* [Salt Lake City: Deseret Book, 2003], 305–6). Perhaps this is why President Ezra Taft Benson felt we were still under condemnation as a church and why just a few years later he urged latter-day saints to flood the earth with the Book of Mormon by making it "more central in our preaching, our teaching, and our missionary work" ("Flood the Earth with the Book of Mormon," 4).

Hopefully by now we have learned our lesson, albeit the hard way, that an inordinate focus on emphasizing common beliefs from the Bible so often leads to neglecting the message of the Restoration and failing in our commission to preach the restored gospel. Such a course offends God and brings us under condemnation. It is encouraging to notice that unlike the previous missionary lesson plans that emphasized "building on common beliefs," *Preach My Gospel* never uses that phrase; instead, it trains missionaries to emphasize the Restoration and teach from the Book of Mormon.

The Path to Apostasy

Not only can efforts to build on common beliefs cause us to neglect the Restoration, they can actually lead to apostasy. This is because it can encourage missionaries to change our doctrines so that they better conform to the beliefs of the world. It is easy for missionaries caught up in the spirit of emphasizing and identifying similarities to take it one step too far and twist our truths and modify our message so as to create common beliefs that don't actually exist. That is, they corrupt restored truth to turn it into common belief.

I saw this happen several times as a missionary, most memorably when my companion emphatically agreed to a Catholic that, just like them, we believed in the Holy Trinity (the doctrine that the Father and the Son are one and the same bodiless being). Not only is this effort misleading, but it also has had serious and severe consequences for the

Church. In fact, it was one of the factors that led the New Testament Christian church to apostasy.

"Some people seem to be embarrassed by the simplicity of the Savior's message," Elder Quentin L. Cook noted. They want to make it "more compatible" with the teachings of the world. "The apostasy occurred in part because of this problem. The early Christians adopted the Greek philosophical traditions, trying to reconcile their own beliefs with the existing culture. The historian Will Durant wrote: 'Christianity did not destroy paganism; it adopted it'" ("Looking beyond the Mark," *Ensign*, March 2003, 42).

This illustrates the danger of trying too hard to be like the world—it is because it just might work! Because they were presumably embarrassed to believe in the uncommon doctrine of a God with a "body of flesh and bones as tangible as man's" (D&C 130:22), early Christians adopted the prevailing Greek view of an impersonal god without body, parts, or passions. In other words, they gave up the doctrine of the true nature of God to fit in with and be accepted by the world. They sold their birthrights as the children of God, created in His image, for the price of popularity. As a result, they achieved exactly what they desired—they became just like everyone else by falling into apostasy just like everyone else. When they did so, they ceased to be the true Church of Jesus Christ.

When we change our doctrine in an attempt to "find common ground" and fit in with the world, we follow the same course that led the New Testament Church into apostasy. "But it will help us be more accepted," some argue. Yes, but at what cost? Are we really willing to become like every other church in order to be treated like them? Are we so ashamed of the fruit from the tree of life that we are willing to give it up in order to be accepted by the great and spacious building and avoid their scorn (see 1 Nephi 8:25–34)? Such compromising of doctrine to fit in and gain popularity led to apostasy once. Would the result be any different if we practiced it now? To paraphrase a quote from the Lord said, "For what is a man profited, if he shall gain the whole world['s approval], and lose his own soul?" (Matthew 16:26).

It is not that establishing common ground is inherently wrong. It is fine to recognize that we have some things in common with other faiths. We do. As Elder Dallin H. Oaks explained, "The Church of Jesus Christ of Latter-day Saints has many beliefs in common with other Christian churches. But we have differences, and those differences explain why we send missionaries to other Christians" ("Apostasy and Restoration," *Ensign*, May 1995, 84). As Elder Oaks demonstrates, we must be quick to follow our similarities with our differences because if we emphasize similarities and downplay differences, then we can give the perception that we are just another Christian church. This is a denial of the Restoration. The other problem is that we distort our doctrine in order to manufacture common ground that in reality does not exist, just so we can fit in with the world. This is the path to apostasy. Perhaps it is because of these inherent dangers that the Lord has *always* cautioned missionaries against the practice of focusing on common beliefs.

Preach My (Restored) Gospel

In an early mission call, the Lord counseled His elders against building on common beliefs and directed them instead to simply preach the restored gospel. In March 1831, the Prophet Joseph Smith extended a mission call to Sidney Rigdon, Parley P. Pratt, and Leman Copley. They were called to serve among the "Shakers," a religious group to which Copley, a recent convert, had formerly belonged. Notice the inspired instruction they received: "Hearken unto my word, my servants Sidney, and Parley, and Leman; for behold, verily I say unto you, that I give unto you a commandment that you shall go and *preach my gospel which ye have received, even as ye have received it*, unto the Shakers" (D&C 49:1; emphasis added).

These missionaries were specifically told by the Lord to preach the restored gospel, the gospel they "[had] received." Not only that, but they were to preach it "even as ye have received it," meaning they were to preach it using latter-day revelation, just as it had been revealed and taught to them.

But then the Lord went even further. To make sure He was clearly understood, the Lord expressly stated that when Leman Copley returned to teach people from his old congregation, he was to "reason with them, *not according to that which he has received of them*, but according to that which shall be taught him by you my servants; and by so doing I will bless him, otherwise he shall not prosper" (D&C 49:4; emphasis added). "That which he has received of them" referred to the gospel truths and religious beliefs he had learned from the Shakers. Though the Shakers shared several common beliefs with the Latter-day Saints, the

Lord specifically counseled Leman Copley *not* to talk about these things in his missionary efforts. In other words, the Lord specifically counseled him against the practice of "building on common beliefs" and "finding common ground;" instead he was directed to teach what he had received from the missionaries of the restored gospel.

We would do well to remember and apply that simple counsel as missionaries. We are not sent out to reason with investigators according to what religious teachings they have already received. Our job is not to focus on our common beliefs. Our commission is to declare the message of the restored gospel, to teach those things the Lord has revealed to us through latter-day revelation to modern prophets. "By so doing [He] will bless [us], otherwise [we] shall not prosper" (D&C 49:4). According to this promise, when we fulfill our commission to preach the restored gospel from latter-day revelation, the Lord will bless us with His Spirit and power, and we will prosper as missionaries.

The Power of Our Position

The promise of spiritual power and success from teaching the restored gospel rather than focusing on common beliefs is perfectly illustrated in the rest of the Joseph Smith story mentioned earlier. Though Sidney Rigdon wasn't willing to declare the message of the Restoration, Joseph Smith was, and the results were remarkable. Parley P. Pratt, who was a witness of the events, gave this account:

> Brother Rigdon spoke first, and dwelt on the Gospel, illustrating his doctrine by the Bible. When he was through, brother Joseph arose like a lion about to roar; and being full of the Holy Ghost, spoke in great power, bearing testimony of the visions he had seen, the ministering of angels which he had enjoyed; and how he had found the plates of the Book of Mormon, and translated them by the gift and power of God. He commenced by saying, "If nobody else had the courage to testify of so glorious a message from Heaven, and of the finding of so glorious a record, he felt to do it, in justice to the people, and leave the event with God."
>
> The entire congregation was astounded; electrified, as it were, and overwhelmed with the sense of the truth and power by which he spoke, and the wonders which he related. A lasting impression was made; many souls were gathered into the fold. And I bear witness, that he, by his faithful and powerful testimony, cleared his garments

of their blood. Multitudes were baptized in Philadelphia and in the regions around; while, at the same time, branches were springing up in Pennsylvania, in Jersey and in various directions. (*Autobiography of Parley P. Pratt* [Salt Lake City: Deseret Book, 1985], 260–61)

Notice the reaction to Joseph Smith's bold testimony of the Restoration. They were "astounded," "electrified," and "overwhelmed" with the "truth and power by which he spoke." And what worked for Joseph will work for us. This is one of the great secrets of missionary work: When we have the courage to teach and testify of the restored gospel, of living prophets and latter-day revelation, of Joseph Smith and the Book of Mormon, then the Lord will pour out His Spirit upon us, and we will teach with the power of God. We will have greater success. We will have more converts and we will have better converts.

When we understand this, we begin to realize why Satan does not want us talking about the Restoration and why he stirs up so many critics to accuse us of worshipping Joseph Smith and of not believing the Bible. It is because he is scared. Satan knows the power of our message, and he does not want it shared. Living prophets and latter-day revelation are a threat to him, and he wants to intimidate us from speaking about them. In days past, that meant mobs and abuse; today, it means criticism and false accusations; it means being marginalized and misinterpreted. But the result Satan seeks is the same: to intimidate us from teaching the message of the Restoration.

The irony of all this is that members of the Church who avoid the message of the Restoration for common ground think they are showing loyalty to Jesus Christ. Because they talk about Jesus Christ exclusively from the Bible, they think they are being faithful disciples. What they don't realize is that the commission to teach the message of the Restoration came from Jesus Christ. It is Christ who wants us talking about Joseph Smith and the Book of Mormon, because they are the great witnesses of Christ in our day. Thus, our loyalty to Jesus Christ today is measured by our loyalty to Joseph Smith and the Restoration. Because the Restoration is Christ's great latter-day work, when we are loyal to it, we are loyal to Him, and when we betray, it we betray him. Those who depart from the message of the Restoration to seek common ground think they are being loyal, but they are being just as disloyal to Christ as were the Pharisees, who were also willing to defend dead prophets and the words of Jehovah but would not stand by the living Christ and the prophets of their day.

The Best Defense Is a Good Offense

We cannot allow ourselves to be manipulated by Satan into avoiding the message of the Restoration. And yet, that is exactly what we are doing when we spend our time emphasizing common beliefs to avoid criticism and persecution. We have allowed ourselves to be distracted from our purpose and have let others control the conversation by becoming reactionary and defensive. We must remember that the best defense is a good offense (see Gordon B. Hinckley, "Pursue the Steady Course," 4).

A perfect example of this is given by Joseph Smith himself in the first verse of Joseph Smith—History. It illustrates how Joseph Smith responded to attacks, not by retreating from the message of the Restoration, but by boldly declaring it. He explained,

> Owing to the many reports which have been put in circulation by evil-disposed and designing persons, in relation to the rise and progress of The Church of Jesus Christ of Latter-day Saints, all of which have been designed by the authors thereof to militate against its character as a Church and its progress in the world—I have been induced to write this history, to disabuse the public mind, and put all inquirers after truth in possession of the facts, as they have transpired, in relation both to myself and the Church, so far as I have such facts in my possession. (JS—H 1:1)

He followed this verse by giving the account of the First Vision, the coming forth of the Book of Mormon, and the restoration of the priesthood. In other words, Joseph Smith's response to attacks on the Restoration was to declare the Restoration. Rather than back down from his claims, he repeated his message more emphatically!

As this verse shows, for Joseph Smith, the best defense was a good offense. Instead of becoming reactionary and endlessly responding to every attack by defensively retreating to the Bible and common beliefs, his response was to simply teach and testify of the Restoration. He was discerning enough to recognize that responding to every critic and trying to justify every doctrine by common belief would only distract him from his purpose and divert him from his message. He recognized that this was a trap, and if he fell for it he would never have time to teach the restored gospel. What if we were wise enough to do the same? What if the next time someone accuses us of worshipping Joseph Smith or not being Christian, we respond by teaching the First Vision? The First Vision would show the proper place of Jesus Christ and Joseph Smith in our faith, and it would show what we believe about Jesus Christ while still being loyal to the Restoration.

Not Common

In the end, what we must remember in all our missionary efforts is that we are not just another Christian church (see *Preach My Gospel*, 7). We are the "only true and living church upon the face of the whole earth" (D&C 1:30). Since this is the case, isn't it a little strange that we try so hard to convince people that our Church is just like theirs? Why do we seek the approval of churches we consider to be wrong? Why do we fight so hard to be accepted by those we are seeking to convert?

The inconsistency of this approach is perhaps best illustrated by a simple analogy mentioned earlier. Imagine a vacuum cleaner salesman trying to sell you a new vacuum in this way: "Here is this new vacuum, and it's just like the one you already have; only, if you buy this one, your family will disown you, and you will need to pay ten percent of your income for the rest of your life. How many would you like to buy?" It doesn't take much sales experience to recognize why that approach wouldn't work very well. And it doesn't work well in missionary work either. We don't need to insult their old vacuum to make the point that the one we offer is like nothing they have ever had before and it is worth whatever price they have to pay to obtain it (see Matthew 13:45–46 and James E. Talmage "Three Parables—The Unwise Bee, the Owl Express, and Two Lamps" *Ensign*, February, 2003, 12–13).

We must remember that the message of the Restoration of the gospel is the most unique and powerful message on earth today. There is nothing common about it. So why do we spend so much time neglecting something so special in favor of emphasizing things so common? We must accept the fact that we are different, and it is in those very differences that we find the source of our strength and the power of our message. It is because we are unique, not the same, that we have a message worth sharing and worth hearing. We seem to have it backward, not realizing that what draws people in to this Church are the differences that we alone have to offer, not the similarities we share in common with other faiths.

"We will never achieve the quantity and quality of converts that [the prophet] and the Lord have envisioned as long as we continue to stress the similarities between us and those of other faiths. It is only when we stress the differences that we are able to make our distinctive contribution in the world and thus make our influence felt" (Bruce R. McConkie, *The Bruce R. McConkie Story*, 305–6).

Accepting Opposition

As we apply this principle, we must accept the fact that the message of the restored gospel will sometimes bring opposition. This has always been the case. Joseph Smith described himself as a "disturber and an annoyer of [Satan's] kingdom" (JS—H 1:20). Moroni warned Joseph that "good and evil" would be spoken of him "among all nations" (JS—H 1:33). So it is that the message of the restored gospel will always have its opponents, but Moroni also promised him that despite the fact that "persecution [would] rage more and more," the Church would still "increase the more opposed, and spread farther and farther" (*Messenger and Advocate* 2:199). Opposition does not hurt us; in fact, it makes us stronger.

This was the lesson President David O. McKay's father learned the hard way that just because something brings opposition does not mean that it should not be shared. What brings the persecution of hell also brings the power of heaven. What attracts criticism also attracts converts. Just because we are accused of worshipping Joseph Smith or not believing the Bible does not mean that we should downplay the Restoration and avoid talking about Joseph Smith and the Book of Mormon. Such a course may bring us more friends, but it yields fewer converts and it offends God. We need to be more concerned with what God thinks of us than what man thinks of us (see D&C 3:7; see also Ezra Taft Benson, "Beware of Pride," *Ensign*, May 1989, 5). As God's true messengers, we must deliver the message He has given us, no matter what the cost or consequence.

As Elder Bruce R. McConkie observed,

> We've got a message, and it ought to be delivered. It's a worldwide message, and our centering should be on Joseph Smith. Here is Joseph

Smith and he revealed Christ, and here is Christ, and here is salvation through this system. That kind of approach will have the effect of dividing people on one hand or on the other, but so you divide them. You divide them—you get some people who are interested. You don't make friends with everyone.

As some of you may recall, President Clark said, "You can't tell the Joseph Smith story without offending people." He said, "We don't need to be so anxiously concerned about not offending the world." And he used the Joseph Smith story as his illustration.

Well, of course you can't. Jesus offended people. Now, we are not trying to offend people but he offended them by the nature of the message that he presented, and we, in my judgment, just have to more affirmatively present our message. (*The Bruce R. McConkie Story*, 303–4)

As we faithfully declare the message of the restored gospel, we will find that what the Lord said of Joseph Smith applies also to the gospel he restored. On the one hand, there will always be opposition to our message. "The ends of the earth shall inquire after thy name, and fools shall have thee in derision, and hell shall rage against thee;" but on the other hand, the message that attracts such fierce criticism also attracts loyal converts—"the pure in heart, and the wise, and the noble, and the virtuous, shall seek counsel, and authority, and blessings constantly from under thy hand. And thy people shall never be turned away from thee by the testimony of traitors" (D&C 122:1–3). May we never be among those who turn away from Joseph Smith; instead, let us, as missionaries, be loyal to the Restoration.

12

OPEN YOUR MOUTH!

In August of 1831, some of the elders of the Church were returning to the East after visiting the land of Zion in Jackson County, Missouri. In their haste to travel home quickly, they made a serious mistake that the Lord rebuked them for. Through this experience, we learn a valuable lesson that provides the final message of this book. To these elders, the Lord declared, "But with some I am not well pleased, for they will not open their mouths, but they hide the talent which I have given unto them, because of the fear of man. Wo unto such, for mine anger is kindled against them" (D&C 60:2).

What had angered the Lord was that, in their haste to return home, these elders had not opened their mouths to share the "talent" they had been given. The word *talent* originally referred to a gold coin and was used by Jesus Christ in a parable in Matthew 25. The main message of that parable was to not hide your "talent," as one of the Lord's servants had done, by burying it in the ground. The Lord reminded us of this parable later on in this revelation, as He made clear what the "talent" was that these elders had buried. He explained, "Behold, they have been sent to preach *my gospel* among the congregations of the wicked; wherefore, I give unto them a commandment, thus: Thou shalt not . . . bury thy talent that it may not be known" (D&C 60:13; emphasis added).

From this it is clear that the "talent" or treasure these elders had been given was the *restored gospel*, and the Lord was upset with them for not opening their mouths and sharing it. As Elder M. Russell Ballard has explained, "Today the voice of the [Lord] is your voice and my voice. And if we are not engaged, many who would hear the message of the Restoration will be passed by" ("Put Your Trust in the Lord," *Ensign*, November 2013, 44). Adding to that thought, Elder L. Tom Perry explained, "No other message has such great eternal significance to everyone living on the earth today. All of us need to teach this message to others with power and conviction. It is the still, small voice of the Holy Ghost that testifies through us of the Restoration, but first we must open our mouths and testify" ("'Bring Souls unto Me,'" 111).

It is a perfect symbol to compare the restored gospel in our lives to a "talent" or treasure because the greatest treasures on earth today are found in the message of the Restoration. It is through the Restoration of the gospel that we can enjoy the Holy Ghost and gifts of the Spirit, eternal marriage and family relationships, the ordinances of salvation and exaltation, the power and authority of the priesthood, and the knowledge of Heavenly Father and Jesus Christ. All the greatest blessings in time and eternity come to us through the Restoration. This is why it upsets the Lord when we don't share this treasure with all who will listen. It angers the Lord when we take the treasure of the Restoration and, like the parable, bury that talent under *common ground*.

One reason that some bury the message of the Restoration under common ground is because they fear that sharing it will offend others. But, as Elder M. Russell Ballard has explained,

> Experience has shown that people are not offended when the sharing is motivated by the spirit of love and concern. . . . It's when we appear only to be fulfilling an assignment and we fail to express real interest and love that we offend others. Don't ever forget, brothers and sisters, that you and I have in our possession the very points of doctrine that will bring people to the Lord. . . We are not just trying to get people to join our Church; we are sharing with them the fulness of the restored gospel of Jesus Christ. ("The Essential Role of Missionary Work," *Ensign*, May 2003, 40)

If we are only pretending to be their friend so we can share the gospel with them, they would be justified in feeling manipulated and offended. But if they know we are truly their friends and that our friendship will not be withdrawn based on their response to the restored gospel, then they will not be offended by a loving invitation. They will understand that what we are sharing comes from our heart and we believe it will bless them with happiness and salvation. Why would anyone be offended by that?

Elder Robert C. Oaks provided a helpful analogy to illustrate why sharing the restored gospel is not as offensive as we have led ourselves to believe.

> Consider that you are invited to a friend's house for breakfast. On the table you see a large pitcher of freshly squeezed orange juice from which your host fills his glass. But he offers you none. Finally, you ask, "Could I have a glass of orange juice?"
>
> He replies, "Oh, I am sorry. I was afraid you might not like orange juice, and I didn't want to offend you by offering you something you didn't desire."
>
> Now, that sounds absurd, but it is not too different from the way we hesitate to offer up something far sweeter than orange juice. I have often worried how I would answer some friend about my hesitancy when I meet him beyond the veil . . . [and he asks me,] "Why have you kept this Book of Mormon, with its message of truth and salvation, a secret?"
>
> My reply, "I was afraid I would damage our friendship," will not be very satisfying to either me or my friend. ("Sharing the Gospel," *Ensign*, November 2000, 81–82)

As this beautiful analogy illustrates, most people are not offended by a sincere invitation, and we can't let the fear of offending them prevent us from trying to save them. As important as it is to be friends with those around us, simply being our friend will not save them. They must accept the restored gospel to be saved in the celestial kingdom. This means that missionary work is not just being friends with our neighbors (that is included in basic discipleship); missionary work is when we open our mouths and share the restored gospel with them. We must have the love and the courage to offer them salvation through the Restoration. Our motto should be the same as the apostle Paul's: "I am not ashamed of the [restored] gospel of Christ: for it is the power of God unto salvation" (Romans 1:16). We must stop burying our message and we must start opening our mouths.

If it upsets the Lord when we bury our message, then, likewise, it must please the Lord whenever we open our mouths to share the restored gospel (see D&C 60:2). This means that, to our Father in Heaven, all of our efforts to share, invite, testify, and teach the restored gospel are always a success. Our success is measured by what we do, not by what others do, and our only real failure in missionary work is the failure to open our mouths and share the message of the Restoration of the gospel of Christ.

Always a Success Story

I learned this lesson in a powerful way from one of my seminary students. One morning, Ashley came into class just beaming with excitement about the news she wanted to share with me. She had been absent from class the day before because of a field trip, and she was thrilled to tell me of the missionary experience she had when she was gone. She explained in detail about how she had met a person, discussed beliefs, and even gave away a copy of the Book of Mormon. Then, after so much enthusiasm and excitement, her countenance fell and her voice softened as she concluded that it was "not a success story" because, in the end, he wasn't very interested.

As I observed and listened to her, my heart broke for her. I wanted to say something to inspire her. I wanted to say something that would encourage her to continue to be the missionary she was and to keep sharing the Book of Mormon, despite this rejection. As I searched for what to say, I silently prayed for words to comfort her. Then, these inspired words left my mouth: "Ashley, every time you open your mouth to share the gospel, it is a success story. If they reject your message, that is a failure on their part, not yours. The only failure for us is when we fail to open our mouths. Whenever you share the restored gospel, it is always a success story!"

I knew as I spoke those words that they were inspired from the Lord, because I had never thought of that before and learned something from what I said. Our success in missionary work is not measured by what others do with our message but by what we do in sharing it. We cannot control the agency of others, so we should not measure our success based on the choices of others. As *Preach My Gospel* states, "Your success as a missionary is measured primarily by your commitment to find, teach, baptize, and confirm people. . . . Remember that people have agency to choose whether to accept your message" (*Preach My Gospel*, 10). This is why Elder Dallin H. Oaks has counseled that "a missionary's goals ought to be based upon the missionary's personal agency and action, not upon the agency or action of others" ("Timing," *Ensign*, October 2003, 15). Consequently, we are personally successful in missionary work whenever we open our mouths to share the gospel, regardless of the outcome. In the end, our only real personal failure as missionaries is the failure to open our mouths and share the message of the Restoration.

A "Real Missionary"

I was taught more about this principle when my oldest son, Bruce, was baptized. For weeks before his baptism, he told me he wanted to be a "real missionary" and invite his friends from school to his baptism. One night, he even shared with me his dream of what it would be like if all his friends came to his baptism and later their whole families joined the Church as a result! He concluded that this would certainly make him a "real missionary."

You can imagine my fatherly concern when the only friends who came to his baptism were already members of the Church. As we were driving home, I asked some questions to see if he was disappointed by his friends not attending. His response was so insightful. It is something every one of us who desires to be a missionary should understand. He said, "Dad, I already knew those friends wouldn't come. When I invited them to my baptism at recess, they said they hated to go to church and didn't want to come. But it's okay, Dad, because now I am like a real missionary. People tell that to the real missionaries all the time."

As my son understood so clearly, our job as missionaries is to invite. It is also to teach and testify. When we do that we are real missionaries, regardless of the response.

Another "real missionary" who had the courage to open her mouth to share the restored gospel was another seminary student I taught named Sharlene. She was part of the high school's premier choir that had been invited to perform at Carnegie Hall in New York with a couple of other high schools from other states. She told me later that she felt that it was no coincidence that her choir had been chosen. They were chosen because "Heavenly Father wanted me to be a missionary," she said. She was so confident of that fact that she packed two copies of the

Book of Mormon and some pass-along cards and was determined to give them away. Over the course of the week, she met and had conversations with several students from the other choirs and became acquainted with one young woman in particular. The subject of religion even came up in one discussion, and she decided that this young woman was someone she needed to give a copy of the Book of Mormon to. I will let Sharlene explain the rest of the story in her own words:

> When we had our last rehearsal, I still hadn't given her the Book of Mormon. The last and only other time I would see her would be onstage, performing. What was I going to do? I decided that it didn't matter what she thought of me; it only mattered what God thought of me, and I knew He would want me to share something very special with her, the Book of Mormon. So I made an observation that our choir robes had baggy, long sleeves. I could hold it in my hand and hide it in my sleeve throughout the concert. That's what I did. The concert was almost two hours long. (Good thing we never needed to clap!) I gave her the Book of Mormon at the end of the concert and told her that it meant so much to me. She said a simple thank you. To this day, I don't know anything that has happened to her, but I hope a seed was planted.

The image of that courageous young woman holding a Book of Mormon in her sleeve for the entire choir performance is an inspiration for the missionary I want to be. What inspires me most about all these member missionary stories is that no one told them to do any of it. This was not an assignment that was given to them or a chore they begrudgingly performed. Something inside them drove them to do this. Something in their hearts compelled them to open their mouths.

I believe that something was their testimonies of the Restoration. It was the conviction that this is the only true Church of Jesus Christ. It was their witness of the Book of Mormon. Because they believed that what they had was so special, they instinctively wanted to share it. I can't help but wonder, would they have had this same missionary desire if they thought our unique beliefs were common among other churches?

Testimony of the Restoration

I believe that one reason that many of us are hesitant to open our mouths as missionaries is that we have not yet caught the vision of the Restoration of the gospel of Jesus Christ and therefore do not fully appreciate what we have to offer to the world. Some seem to have convinced themselves that our message is ordinary and our beliefs are common. But there is nothing common about our message. "Our message is unique," proclaimed Elder L. Tom Perry. "We declare to the world that the fulness of the gospel of Jesus Christ has been restored to the earth" ("The Message of the Restoration," *Ensign*, May 2007, 88).

What we have to offer is unique and special. It is found nowhere else in all the world. What has been restored to us is the true Church and gospel of Jesus Christ. It is nothing less than the one true path to salvation. It is a message that everyone needs to hear. It is the pearl of great price that is worth whatever sacrifice it takes to obtain it and to share it (Matthew 13:45–46). Only when that conviction of that burns in our hearts will we have the courage to open our mouths.

As Elder M. Russell Ballard has explained, "Our love for the Lord and appreciation for the Restoration of the gospel are all the motivation we need to share" our message ("Creating a Gospel-Sharing Home," 84). Just like when we really enjoy a good movie we naturally want to tell everyone to go see it, so it is with the message of the Restoration. The more that message burns in our hearts, the more it changes and converts and blesses us, the more we will want to share it with others. This is why I believe a missionary's effectiveness is directly related to his or her testimony of, conversion to, and love of the message of the Restoration of the gospel of Jesus Christ (see Joseph B. Wirthlin, "The Book of Mormon: The Heart of Missionary Proselyting," 14).

A few years ago, I was asked to teach some future missionaries about how to prepare for their missions. I taught some of the principles that I have emphasized in this book. When I was done, I concluded with words that I had not prepared to say. These words, I feel, make a fitting conclusion to this book. Pointing to the missionary nametag I was wearing as an object lesson, I said,

> In a few years, many of you will receive a nametag like this, but this is not what makes you a missionary. What makes you a missionary is deeper than a nametag; it is what is underneath the nametag, in your heart, that makes you a missionary. If you want to *become* a missionary, what you need to do is take Joseph Smith—History and the Book of Mormon and read them. Then, when you're done, read them again. Then read them again and again and again. Read until your heart is filled with the testimony of the message of the Restoration. Read until

you know that the gospel of Jesus Christ has been restored through the Prophet Joseph Smith. When that message burns in your heart like fire, when your desire to share it is so strong that it outweighs the fear to open your mouth, when you love it so much that you can't *not* share it with whoever will listen, then you have the heart of a missionary. Then you have *become* a missionary of the restored gospel.

Becoming a Missionary of the Restored Gospel

The purpose of this book is to inspire us to become missionaries of the restored gospel by sharing first things first when sharing the gospel. As we have seen, becoming a missionary of the restored gospel means understanding that there is nothing common about our message. Therefore, Restoration missionaries are not content just establishing common ground but rather are determined to proclaim the good news of the Restoration of the gospel of Jesus Christ. For them, the Restoration is the very source of their power and purpose (see chapter 1).

Missionaries of the restored gospel are First Vision missionaries. They take their investigators in the quickest and most direct route to the Sacred Grove. Like Joseph Smith, they teach the First Vision first (see chapter 2).

Missionaries of the restored gospel are Book of Mormon missionaries. They use the Book of Mormon to prove that this Church is true by inviting all to read and pray about it. They have full confidence that God will confirm the truth of it by the power of the Holy Ghost. They recognize that the Book of Mormon is the most powerful resource they have in conversion (see chapters 3 and 4).

Missionaries of the restored gospel boldly and humbly declare that this is the only true Church of Jesus Christ. They recognize that our mission is not to try to convince the world that ours is just another Christian church but rather to proclaim that the true Church of Jesus Christ has been restored (see chapter 5).

Missionaries of the restored gospel don't Bible bash. They know that the Bible is not common ground; it is battleground and has been for centuries. They know how ineffective it is to try to prove the Church true from the Bible because everyone interprets it differently. Instead of arguing about the Bible, they rely on latter-day revelation (see chapter 6).

Missionaries of the restored gospel know that because of the Apostasy, the Bible is a sealed book, and the key to unlocking it is latter-day revelation. Therefore, they introduce their investigators to the scriptures and revelations of the Restoration and the gift of the Holy Ghost so that they can unlock and understand the Bible for themselves (see chapter 7).

Missionaries of the restored gospel understand that Joseph Smith is the Prophet of the Restoration and the great revealer of Christ in our day. They trust in and follow the Savior's declaration that "this generation shall have my word through [Joseph Smith]" (D&C 5:10). They know that the names of Jesus Christ and Joseph Smith are united together in our message to the world (see chapter 8).

Missionaries of the restored gospel are not deceived by the trap that they must choose between new revelation and old revelation or between Joseph Smith and Jesus Christ. They choose to believe in and proclaim both as they testify of the living Christ who speaks today through living prophets. They know that the issue is not whether Mormons believe in the biblical Jesus but whether the world today will believe in and accept *the living Christ* (see chapter 9).

Missionaries of the restored gospel know that the things of God are known only by the Spirit of God. They invite all to ask of God to find out for themselves by the power of the Holy Ghost, rather than by physical evidence or intellectual reasoning. They trust that the Lord's sheep will hear His voice and let the Spirit do the work in missionary work (see chapter 10).

Missionaries of the restored gospel are loyal to the Restoration. They do not avoid the Restoration by seeking safety in common beliefs because they know this offends God and brings us under condemnation. In the face of opposition and criticism, they continue to teach the message of the Restoration, knowing that the best defense is a good offense (see chapter 11).

Missionaries of the restored gospel open their mouths! They know that the message of the Restoration is a treasure they must never bury under common ground, and that their only real failure in missionary work is the failure to share this message: The gospel of Jesus Christ has been restored today through the Prophet Joseph Smith (see chapter 12).

My hope is that these words might inspire all of us to become missionaries of the restored gospel and that it might encourage each of us to go forward in faith and share the greatest message in all the world—that Christ lives and His Gospel has been restored!

ABOUT THE AUTHOR

Mark Mathews has served as a teacher in the Church Educational System for over ten years, working full-time for the seminaries and institutes of religion and part-time as an adjunct BYU religion professor. He has BS and MS degrees in marriage and family studies from Brigham Young University and a PhD in education from Utah State University. He is the author of several articles including "Satan's Rebellion" (*Ensign*, March 2015) and "God's Plan for Families" (*Ensign*, July 2015). Originally from Kingwood, Texas, he now lives with his wife and five children in Brigham City, Utah.